Surrender Y

Inspiring Stories of Women Releasing Trauma

A Green Heart Living Press Anthology

Robin H. Clare and Elizabeth B. Hill
with Amy Jaffe Barzach, Colleen Brunetti,
Paulomi Campbell, Mary Constance, Holly Dudash,
Lowri Foyle, Charmaine Harkins, Angelika Kilian,
Shell Sawyer, Karina Viante-Phelan,
Kristie K. Warren, and Bryanne Weightman

GREEN HEART
LIVING
— PRESS —

Surrender Your Story
Copyright © 2022 Robin H. Clare
All rights reserved. No part of this book may be used or reproduced by any means, graphic, electronic, or mechanical, including photocopying, recording, taping or by any information storage retrieval system without the written permission of the publisher, except in the case of brief quotations embodied in critical articles and reviews.

ISBN (paperback): 978-1-954493-37-7
Cover design: Barb Pritchard of Infinity Brand Design and Elizabeth B. Hill

This book is designed to provide information and motivation to our readers. It is sold with the understanding that the publisher is not engaged to render any type of psychological, legal, or any other kind of professional advice. The content of each article is the sole expression and opinion of its author, and not necessarily that of the publisher. No warranties or guarantees are expressed or implied by the publisher's choice to include any of the content in this volume. Neither the publisher nor the individual author(s) shall be liable for any physical, psychological, emotional, financial, or commercial damages, including, but not limited to, special, incidental, consequential or other damages. Our views and rights are the same: You are responsible for your own choices, actions, and results.

Dedication

To all those healing trauma and
writing the next chapters of their lives.

Table of Contents

Dear Reader,

We hold our stories with us

In our hearts

Our heads

Our bodies

The stories can become who we are

When we turn these stories into words

Our stories are honored and released

The world carries our stories with us

We are no longer alone

As our stories are so held

They lose their power *over* us

And we find our power *through* them

Thank you for holding our stories with us

May you grow your power *through* them, with us

Love & Transformation,
Elizabeth

Introduction
Robin H. Clare

On New Year's Day each year, I do a special meditation to ask my spirit guides, "What would you like me to learn this year?" In past years, the request has been to study a specific healing modality or learn to live in the present moment. During this year's meditation, I heard a single voice say, " Surrender your story." I replied, "Which story?" The voice answered, "All of them."

The response so amused me that I shared the experience with my friend and colleague, Elizabeth Hill. Because we each have a lifetime of stories that have influenced everything from our relationships, health, work, and how we see the world, we agreed that this topic would be an outstanding anthology.

What are the origins of our stories that we need to surrender? I believe that they result from unhealed trauma that has morphed into a state of suffering. This unhealed trauma or woundedness can have many origins, but the most relatable would be due to something that was said or done to you or not receiving what you most need in life.

The fourteen authors you will meet in *Surrender Your Story* have experienced traumatic events, found the courage to heal their suffering, welcomed the grace of healing, and are brave enough to share their surrender stories with you. It is our wish that you find yourself in our rich stories and become inspired to heal your life and serve others on your path.

Chapter 1

Celebrate Life

Amy Jaffe Barzach

For years, "deal with loss by celebrating life" was the story I told myself and how I found the strength to go on after the death of my son Jonathan. This seemingly simple phrase was a lifeline for me. You could find it on a piece of paper with Jonathan's picture in my pocket. I repeated it to myself in the shower when I wasn't sure I could live without him. It helped me keep my head above water when waves of grief crashed over me.

Jonathan was born with sparkling blue "old soul" eyes and a beautiful smile. The year he was born, I thought I had it all—a loving husband, two happy and healthy boys (Jonathan and Daniel, three years older), wonderful family and friends, two sweet dogs, a successful career, and an almost six-month maternity leave. Two weeks before Jonathan was born, the local newspaper even featured my "perfect life" in a half-page article entitled "Women Who Have It All and Have It Good." In the pictures, I was eight months pregnant in my downtown Hartford office, relaxing with my husband in front of a roaring fire, wearing a clown nose as I played with Daniel, and exercising. That spring and summer, my family enjoyed life.

Then one day, Jonathan couldn't hold his head up. It took us months to figure out what was wrong, and later that fall, he was diagnosed with spinal muscular atrophy. The doctors thought he had Type II, the less terrible kind. We made a promise to Jonathan that we would help him have a good life, despite the challenges of this disease. The doctors were wrong. Eight weeks later, they changed his diagnosis to Type I and told us he would die before his second birthday. Life as we knew it was over. When Jonathan died less than two weeks later, the days were difficult, the nights were worse, and the mornings only brought more days.

Honoring Jonathan

After Jonathan's diagnosis was changed to terminal just before Christmas, a hospice counselor suggested we think of something we could do in his honor, something that would make him smile. We remembered being at the park and seeing a little girl in a wheelchair, sadly watching everyone else play on a playground she couldn't get to or play on. We imagined that in Jonathan's dreams, he would want playgrounds to be places where everyone could play, regardless of ability or disability.

We decided to develop a playground where children with and without disabilities could play together. The hospice counselor encouraged us to think about the essence of the idea and share that with Jonathan. The heart of our concept was a place where children of all abilities could celebrate life—which gave my husband Peter and me many potential ways to make it happen. After Jonathan's death in January 1995, we wanted to move forward with a memorial project in his honor, but the brutally honest truth is that I felt and was lost for months.

Most people run from grief or try to stay busy, so they don't notice it. For a long time, I did both. At first, I tried to be the perfect "bereaved mother"—goodness knows what this means. I wanted to make it all better for the people I cared about who were also feeling lost. After Jonathan's death, I unconsciously decided to take the fork in the road toward service. When I think about a meaningful life, the things I did after Jonathan's death—in his honor—helped me recover and gave me a reason to go on. I dealt with this devastating loss by creating opportunities for others to celebrate life and making communities more inclusive, one playground at a time.

We started with Jonathan's Dream in West Hartford, Connecticut, which was then one of the first inclusive playgrounds in the country. Ultimately, we helped more than 135 communities in 25 states develop playgrounds where children of all abilities could play, learn and celebrate life together. My focus was on making a difference. It was all about celebrating life and creating meaning from Jonathan's death—for others, for communities, and for Jonathan to keep his memory alive. I didn't realize that this applied to me too.

Learning to Receive

After Jonathan's death, my way of dealing with loss by celebrating life was to, like a lighthouse, shine a light for others. To be a light that helped guide others back to safe waters—from their own grief to how they could make a difference. Sometimes in life, we can be a lighthouse for our family, friends, community, and people in need. And when we are lost, a lighthouse can represent the idea that others can be there for us. I believe in reciprocity—relationships being about give and take—but I was always more comfortable being the person to give.

Knowing how good it feels to give to others, why has it been so hard for me to be the person who receives? Even though we may feel alone and devastated by the trials, tribulations, and even tragedies of life, we have to keep going; we have to find a way back to the lighthouses in our lives. There is strength and comfort in figuring out what matters to you. What energizes you? What drains you? Give yourself permission to put yourself into the equation of your own life. The very things I thought I didn't have the strength or courage to deal with were the very things that were sapping my energy or making me feel more afraid, more vulnerable, and more lost. Once I faced them, embraced them, and even imagined myself dancing with them, I was able to survive them and even thrive because of them.

Many years ago, over a glass of wine at a pub near Princeton University, a colleague taught me that the Latin derivation of the word "pretend" means to hold true, act as if it is true, and as a result, make it true. For example, with this definition, I could act as if I was courageous when I felt afraid and, as a result, feel more courageous. With this concept, you can overcome almost anything. You can also find people to be role models for you—people you know or can meet in person or people you can meet through books, media, or research.I found this concept very helpful and encourage you to try it. In addition to being gateways to healing, the surprising truth is that powerful emotions like grief and despair (though admittedly uninvited) can be effective ways to access our creativity, energy, and deepest longings.

Facing Grief

Pretending to be brave was enough until the day it wasn't. That day, I was brought to my knees again, exactly how I felt the day Jonathan died. Once again, I didn't think I had the strength or the courage I needed to go on. I was afraid that if I faced my grief, if I permitted myself to pay attention to my own needs, desires, and interests, to dare to think that I—myself—also deserved to celebrate life—the grief that was there might swallow me whole, and I might never find my way back.

For me, there will always be a "before"—during our son Jonathan's life and an "after"—after his death. I felt like a boat on the water being buffeted by unrelenting waves. If I gave up my grief, I was afraid I would lose my connection to Jonathan. The person I was before Jonathan's death—I didn't know who this person was anymore. And what was left if the grief and the dealing with loss by celebrating life (for others) were gone?

Grief is both devastating and transformative. It is natural to want to ignore it, but when we do, the result is often an inability to feel anything. Powerful learning can come from grief if/when we let it. In moments of significant loss, we have access to tremendous clarity about what really matters. I invite you to have compassion for yourself. You may be on a path you would never have chosen, but I encourage you to make the most of it if you are on it. Give yourself permission to put yourself into the equation of your own life.

The story that I am ready to surrender is that honoring Jonathan's life and death and dealing with loss by celebrating life means that there isn't a place for me in the equation. I teach students in The Women's Advancement Initiative LEAD program at the University of Hartford about permission to say yes to opportunities and challenges (inspired by my mentor, Mims Butterworth, former president of Hartford College for Women). It is equally important, however, for all of us to give ourselves permission to put our own needs, desires, and preferences into the equation of our lives.

I didn't realize it then, but I have been teaching students exactly what I needed to learn for years. When you have spent so many years of your life thinking of others, putting "service above self," as Rotary says, and dedicating yourself to making the world a better place in big and small ways, it can be easy to forget or not even know what your own needs, desires, and preferences are.

Putting Yourself Into the Equation

Putting yourself into the equation of your own life means continuing to make a difference, continuing to care about others, *and* realizing that you matter too. Just like the oxygen masks on airplanes that you have to put on yourself before you help the person next to you, you have to invest in and make yourself a priority. As I surrender my story about service for others first and that there isn't room for me in the equation of my life, I am now ready to embrace the fact that I can do both. I can continue on the path I took toward service, *and* this fork in the road can merge with the path toward my own self-actualization. Each of us needs to put ourselves into the equation of our lives. And I not only have permission to do this, but I also *have* to do this. If you don't take care of yourself, you cannot sustain yourself to be of service to others.

Years after Jonathan's death, people who see me at the University of Hartford or doing keynote speeches at conferences sometimes wonder how my husband Peter and I survived Jonathan's death. They say they don't know how they would have gotten through it. *Accidental Courage, Boundless Dreams* is the title of the first book I wrote. At the time, I loved the title because I felt like my courage was accidental, mostly because I didn't know where it had come from. I didn't think of myself as particularly strong or brave. In hindsight, though, I would like to change the title to "Choosing Courage, Boundless Dreams" because I now realize that within each of us are the seeds of what we need in life—strength, courage, discipline, hope—everything. Much like mighty oak trees growing from little acorns, I now know each of us can choose to be courageous or anything else we need to be.

To help me remember this, I carry a small acorn charm in my pocket. I am a big believer in symbols. I love the acorn metaphor so much that in The Women's Advancement Initiative LEAD program, we give silver acorn pocket charms to students to help them remember their strengths and their potential. I also believe that threads connect us to what matters and to other people. Our program is proud to celebrate and continue the legacy of Hartford College for Women for today's students. I was delighted when I learned a few years ago that when the predecessor of Hartford College for Women was established in 1933, an acorn was planted to symbolize the potential of what was then a "noble experiment"—educating women. I don't think it is an accident. This sisterhood across time connects today's students to the legacy of Hartford College for Women. Acorns are a symbol that binds both of these parts of my life.

Celebrating Life

The unrelenting waves sometimes still crash over me—*and*—there is much more distance between the waves and many more good days, weeks, months, and even years. Sometimes, the overwhelming and unrelenting waves are back on the anniversary of Jonathan's birth, death, or random days. On those days, I give myself permission to feel whatever I am feeling because I know that Jonathan is always with me in my heart and that it is possible to find the good in grief. I can also tell you that what I learned through the grieving and healing process made me a better person, a more compassionate person, a person who knows what really matters. So, in this next chapter of my life, I, too, am celebrating life!

Here is how you can start: Pay attention to what energizes and drains you. If you think you have to do something right away about the things that drain you, it is human nature not to notice them. I invite you to give yourself a window of time to pay attention (a month, or a season...) Be sure to record your observations of what drains you and what energizes you. Then after the window of time is over, review your observations and look for patterns and themes. Pick one of the things that energizes you and do it more. Then look at the list of what drains you and start by looking for one tiny micro change you could make to eliminate something that drains you. Make yourself a priority.

What do you want to say no to? What do you want to make time for? By finding ways to put yourself more into the equation of your life, you can celebrate life for the greater good, for others, and for yourself.

The college students I work with at the University of Hartford are wrestling with their own trials, tribulations, and even tragedies. Yet, they come to college determined to live their dreams, to make the most of their time in college. College life compounded by health, financial, and familial challenges can be overwhelming. Perhaps when my students and I permit ourselves to surrender our stories, we can translate the energy our stories once held and use this as catalysts to achieve our hopes and dreams. The first step to genuinely celebrating life is giving ourselves permission to put ourselves into the equations of our lives.

"The very things I thought I didn't have the strength or courage to deal with were the very things that were sapping my energy or making me feel more afraid, more vulnerable, and more lost. Once I faced them, embraced them, even imagined myself dancing with them, I was able to not only survive them but even thrive because of them."

Amy Jaffe Barzach

About Amy Jaffe Barzach

Amy Jaffe Barzach is the Executive Director of The Women's Advancement Initiative (WAI) at the University of Hartford. Proud to celebrate and continue the legacy of Hartford College for Women (HCW), WAI positions women for success through education and leadership programs, research and scholarship opportunities, and career connections and experiences.

Prior to joining the University of Hartford, Amy was the founder and executive director of Boundless Playgrounds, the first national nonprofit dedicated to helping communities create inclusive playgrounds. During her tenure, Boundless Playgrounds helped 135 communities in 25 states develop inclusive playgrounds where children, with and without disabilities, could play, learn, and celebrate life together. The first Boundless playground, Jonathan's Dream, was developed in memory of Amy and Peter Barzach's son, Jonathan.

Author Contact Information:
www.hartford.edu/womensadvancement
amyjaffebarzach@gmail.com
860-983-5040

Chapter 2

Find Your People, Pick Your Fights, and Shine Your Light

Colleen Brunetti

Find Your People

When we think of a trauma, we most often think of a singular event, like a car accident or a natural disaster. Or we think of trauma as caused by another person's acts that harm us in significant ways, be it a random stranger or an ongoing toxic relationship. But what happens if the trauma first comes from inside us—when our body fails us in unexpected ways? In a culture where the trope is, "If you have your health, you have everything," how do you process the trauma of what feels like having your body betray you?

I was 28 years old when my world flipped upside down with a major health diagnosis. Before that, I was building my American dream. I had attended a great college, then gotten a Master's degree, built a career path as a teacher with leadership aspirations, and had just had a baby and bought a house. However, all was not right. I never recovered full physical functioning after the birth of my son. As months passed, I became increasingly short of breath during everyday tasks.

At the top of the stairs at work, I would have to go and hide around the corner, sit on a bench, and try to suck in enough oxygen to steady my breathing and slow my heart rate. I had always been athletic, dancing was my sport, and I loved the gym. But now, I found myself in what I thought was a desperately out-of-shape state, a condition I blamed on post-partum sleeplessness and baby weight.

After nearly passing out trying to come up from my basement and a series of viral lung infections, a trip to the ER earned me a chest x-ray. The next day at work, I checked my voicemail, only to be told in a message that, "Your heart is a little enlarged, it's probably no big deal, but you should see a cardiologist."

And so began my nightmare. That enlarged heart turned out to be a very big deal. It would prove to be a physical manifestation of a rare lung disease called pulmonary arterial hypertension (PH), and Dr. Google told me I had, at best, two-to-five years to live.

On January 2, 2008, that diagnosis was my first foray into medical trauma, though it would be many years until I learned to call it for what it was and even longer to come to understand that I have PTSD from the experiences that I would go on to have because of PH.

At just 28 years old, I was dying. Doctors looked at me with deep sympathy and furrowed brows. Well-meaning family and friends didn't know what to say when I told them bluntly what the prognosis likely was. I spiraled. I paced the house late into the night. I cried constantly; I lost my job when the district I worked in decided they didn't want a sick teacher, no matter how talented, and made it impossible to stay. More than anything, I worried I would not live long enough to see my toddler son, now 15 months old, even reach Kindergarten.

My first rays of hope in those early dark days came from other patients I met online. They supported and loved me, but they challenged me too. I had so much about my mindset that I needed to change, from surrendering to needing to take copious amounts of medication when I was used to living a holistic lifestyle to learning that life was still sweet between the hard parts.

Within the first few years of my diagnosis, I was handed a book by Dr. Bernie Siegel entitled *Love, Medicine, and Miracles*. Dr. Siegel was an oncology surgeon at Yale, and in this book, he takes a deep dive into what makes a survivor in the face of something not thought to be survivable. Further, he spoke of death with such candor and of living whatever life you have left with purpose and intention.

His wisdom was life-changing for me. The grief, anger, denial, and confusion after a major medical diagnosis are genuine, authentic, and okay to go through. In fact, you *have to* go through it. But if you stay in that state of mind too long, whatever life you have left will pass you by. I wasn't about to let that happen.

I didn't want to miss a thing, and so I began the mindset shift of living life as fully as possible, no matter how much time I had left. Living with intention took on a whole new, very pressed-for-time meaning. Now I try to be that voice of steady reason for other patients, especially those newly diagnosed. As the saying goes, "You have survived 100% of your hardest days." And I want people to think, *So what can I do to make the most of the days that are still coming?*

I believe with my whole soul that I could not have survived those early days without those tough life lessons from those who had already been there. Where the mind goes, the body follows, and my mind was not in fighting shape. I am thankful that I learned to find my people in the early months of my diagnosis. No matter what you're facing, try to do the same. Find your people. Let them carry you. Then go and do the same for others.

Pick Your Fights

While I choose joy (most days!), life as a chronically ill patient is not easy. The American for-profit healthcare system is broken and crumbling more by the day. Part of living with intention is navigating that and standing up to it when you have to.

Medications cannot be picked up at your local pharmacy for a rare disease like PH. Instead, they are mail delivered through a cumbersome and complex specialty pharmacy system. They are incredibly costly, and mine run about $250,000 a year. Insurance helps, but not often enough.

Even if you have "good" insurance, the co-pays can be so astronomical that additional financial assistance often has to be secured. Simply figuring out how to afford your medications and get all the pieces lined up can become a part-time job, especially around the first of the year when high deductible plans turn over and everything is out of pocket until that deductible is met.

In addition to the financial stress, there is the system itself. Specialty pharmacies and insurance corporations can be a nightmare to navigate. This isn't some mild medication we're waiting on through all of this; it's the life-saving stuff that we will die without, sometimes in a matter of days to hours (no exaggeration!), depending on the drug.

When things go wrong, it's almost instantly an emergency of some sort. When they go wrong over and over again, I have found that I have developed both anticipatory rage and also a kind of grief over having to be in a constant state of fight. It's exhausting and steals quality of life, which is so precious.

It now can manifest itself as PTSD, as I recently experienced sitting on my couch, heart fluttering, and pre-crying as I tried to psych myself up for another battle call I had to place. While it's hard to go through, understanding that what I am feeling is authentic and okay and a part of the process (even though I hate it!) has been freeing.

Like many women, I was conditioned to hold back my big feelings. We are told not to be so emotional, so bossy, or worse, so shrill. We need to leave those harmful messages behind and step into our power, and claim our rights. This shift did not come easy. I'm softspoken and an empath at heart. Definitely not a fighter by nature, but it is well past time women claimed their power and found their voice, especially in matters of human rights, as I believe healthcare is (or should be).

I had a singular event that pushed me to this point, and I remind myself of it often because it helps me remember that standing up for myself is okay and right. At the time, I was fighting an ongoing medication delivery issue, where medications were not showing up when they should have, and I was running out. At that time, I was required to sign for the delivery so I was also stuck at home, and when the specialty pharmacy failed again to deliver the medications as promised for a third time, I missed my now preschool son's holiday party.

I was devastated. I still didn't know how long I would have with him, how long he would have his Mommy to be there, and this corporation stole my moment with him. As I sputtered on the phone with yet another manager, I told her what the corporation had caused to happen.

In what was surely an attempt at empathy, she kindly said, "I understand. I'm a mom too, and I'm sorry." Something about that intended kindness made me snap. I fired back, "Yes, but you're pretty much guaranteed to see your kid grow up. I am not. And I missed this."

I heard her suck in her breath. We closed the conversation, I snapped my cell phone shut (not nearly as satisfying as banging down an old-fashioned receiver), and I burst into tears. All the while, I had that voice of doubt in my head. *Was I too harsh on her?*

Was I overreacting? Should I have been more polite? It was only a little preschool event, after all.

Minutes later, I opened up my computer and saw on social media that a fellow patient I was fond of had died unexpectedly. The tears started fresh. I WAS justified in my fight and my words. My friend was gone. Her time was done. Her family was shattered without her. And nobody, no company, no individual, had the right to steal my time with my son from me.

This lit something inside me that still burns today. I would go on to pursue advocacy, starting with my own disease state, and then on to rare disease and chronic illness in general.

This side of health care is not medical trauma in the way we think of more typical physical or emotional trauma from a difficult medical event. Instead, it is psychological trauma brought on by a very broken, for-profit system. The people on the other end of the phone are well-meaning enough. I try never to yell at them (and am successful at least most of the time), and often they are also powerless in the same tangled mess I am.

What right do companies have to steal our time and energy with repeated human error, bankrupt us because we had the audacity to become ill in America, risk our lives when things go wrong, and we don't have medication in hand as expected and offer up sub-par customer service through it all? Until we hold the companies accountable with real-world stories about their negative impact and get our legislators in linked arms with us to pass fundamental laws that affect real change, it will keep happening. This is a fight I am in, and I choose it every day because I believe it's right and gives purpose to my journey, which is hard far too often.

Every time I call my representatives, every email I write to them, every time I post my stories on social media, and with every media interview I do, I am choosing to release a story that could make me a victim and choose instead to make it an opportunity for empowerment and change. We should all be in this fight together.

All of us are victims of the American healthcare system in some way (and many of us have also benefited greatly, so it's important not to brush that aside). All of us are a split second away from a catastrophic condition of our own. What happens to us in life is not guaranteed. But how we respond is always a choice, and how we pick the issues we deem worth fighting for matters.

Shine Your Light

When I look back on my advocacy efforts over the years, I am a little stunned at all that I've been able to accomplish. I remember how I was once a soft-spoken teacher who preferred to shut her classroom door, attend to her students, and stay out of the spotlight. I remember that, like most of the population, public speaking was one of the scariest things I could imagine doing.

Now I have gone in front of specialty pharmacy companies, sometimes to call them out on their mess, and other times to work with them to build on what works well. I've trained employees of pharmaceutical companies on what it's like to live as a patient with the disease their drugs help, and often I'm the first patient they've ever met. To see the light go on as they understand the impact of their work from a first-person story is immensely rewarding.

I've stood (shaking in my stilettos) in front of the FDA to convince them they should care about studying the patient experience in pulmonary hypertension. I followed that up with being invited back to speak again...twice! In addition, I have testified in front of committees for my state's legislature a number of times and worked with a state rep to help pass a law to protect patients from predatory billing practices from health insurance companies.

I've visited Capitol Hill in Washington and spoken to legislative aides numerous times, working on getting their bosses (my reps—they work for me, and you!) to co-sign on to important bills that will further protect patients at a national level. I've been featured in magazines, newspapers, and television spots, amplifying the message to the general public. I am also proud to say that I wrote a book called *Defining the New Normal: A Guide to Becoming More than Your Diagnosis*, which is available on Amazon.

I have traveled the world speaking to other patients, sometimes to audiences of over 1,000 people. Connecting with other patients and helping them see that they can create their path despite this diagnosis is the most rewarding thing I know. So why do I talk about all this? It's not to trumpet my success. Instead, it's to encourage you. Believe me, I did not have *any* of the skills needed to accomplish all these things the day I was diagnosed.

What I did have was passion, a voice, a deep sense of justice, and a little bit of an Irish temper. And more importantly, I had the right people around me—my fellow patients for sure. Staff at the Pulmonary Hypertension Association saw something in me and pushed me right off the cliff of my comfort zone, urging me to do more and giving me the tools to do it. My family—loving me and being my biggest cheerleader.

I know you can make a change, too, no matter what you've been through. There is so much in this life we cannot plan for, and so much we will face. It's part of the human experience. But we always get to choose our response. Along the way, you'll never know what joy you will experience.

That baby boy I feared I wouldn't be there for? He's 16 now and a high school junior. We went on to adopt a baby girl, and she's now eight. So I didn't see one kid through to Kindergarten—I saw two. And now, I fully intend to see them both graduate. I also found my way to a new career. I picked up an old passion for writing and for art and have been creating. I've met the most incredible people. Life has been sweet, despite the hardest parts.

If you can take the bad and turn it into something good, stand up for yourself, and ease the path for others, what may still be a tragedy can turn into triumphs you cannot even dream of. But, of course, this isn't to say the hard parts won't still be with you.

I can't stress enough that it's okay to feel those, too, and to honor any grief and trauma processing (or any other emotions) you must go through, no matter how long or how many times you have to do it. To deny that process that would be so harmful. But don't stay there too long. Find that passion. Use your voice. Shine your light.

"It doesn't matter what life throws at you.
What matters is how you choose to respond."

Colleen Brunetti

About Colleen Brunetti

Colleen Brunetti, M.Ed., C.H.C., is an author and rare disease advocate. Diagnosed with a rare debilitating lung disease called pulmonary hypertension (PH) in 2008, she has dedicated her life to fighting to make the healthcare system work better for patients and to inspire others to take a stand. She recently completed two years as Chair of the Board of Trustees for the Pulmonary Hypertension Association and is a noted speaker and political advocate at the local and national levels.

When not taking on the system, Colleen writes, illustrates, and publishes children's books and works as a coach to launch other aspiring authors. She lives in Connecticut with her husband, two kids, and a small zoo of four-legged family members.

Author Contact Information:
www.ColleenBrunetti.com

Chapter 3

My Most Genuine Life

Paulomi Campbell

I was born in Mumbai, India, to two medical doctors who migrated to America to give their children (myself and my brother) opportunities they never had. The inherent expectation was that my brother and I should achieve more than they did because of their sacrifices to leave their families in India and move to a foreign country. This was never said aloud, but it was clear that the expectation was to achieve everything they did and more.

Providing Context

My mother is the most determined person I have ever met. She overcame many obstacles in her life and felt her ticket out of poverty was to be a medical doctor and move to America. Yet, she never lost sight of her goals. She worked hard and not only learned how to cook and serve others, but she would stay up late at night, sacrificing sleep so she would be the first in her class.

She was so clear on her goals that nothing could get in her way. She achieved everything she had set her mind to. Then I came along. Saying she was unprepared for a child like me is an understatement. She got a daughter who was completely opposite from her. I was and still am a free spirit. As a child, I was not particularly driven academically, and on top of that, I was not clear on what my path would be. I honestly did not care because all I wanted was to have fun and for people to like me.

This was not ok for my mom and not ok with the South-Asian culture I was a part of. After all, we are considered the "model minority," contributing significantly to science, math, or engineering. I did not fit into this box in the slightest. The expectation was to follow a specific path; in my case, it was medical school, residency, not necessarily a fellowship because it was important to get married at a certain age so that I would not miss the "right" age to have children.

Any deviation from this life trajectory was considered not only disobedient to my parents, but to the community and culture at large. As a result of being "different" I constantly felt the pressure to "be good." I felt compelled to hide the reality of who I was, even from myself. I would follow my honors humanities friends, pretending to be interested in school. I even went so far as to change my grades so that my parents thought I was getting straight A's.

Choosing to Belong

I showed up with so many layers to the world that it was hard for me even to keep up. Deep inside, I felt lost, confused, ashamed, lonely, and never good enough. I existed in this space for many years. On the surface, I looked happy, distracting myself from my pain by constantly focusing on receiving attention from friends and men. If other people, especially a man, liked me/chose me, I felt ecstatic. But, like any addiction, I needed more and more to hide the pain I felt deep down inside.

If I felt rejected or not chosen, I would become highly anxious and start searching for another man's attention to fill that void. This need to be worthy enough to be chosen by a man was so strong that at age 26, I decided to get married to someone that I barely even knew. He liked me and wanted to marry me, and that's all I needed at the time to say yes. My now ex-husband did not know my history.

He did not know that I only said yes to him because I wanted to show my college ex-boyfriend that I had moved on after he strung me along for years. He did not know that I had failed out of three colleges and moved to D.C. on a whim, thinking this would help me escape my pain. He did not know that I said yes to him because he was from the same region in India that I was from. I thought that by marrying him, I would finally make my parents and the community I grew up in less embarrassed of me. I would finally belong.

The Sting of Divorce

I thought being the first person in my community to get married would redeem me. But instead, it ended in the worst possible outcome, at least in the eyes of my parents and the community I grew up in: divorce. I left my ex-husband after four months of marriage and now felt like I was permanently stamped with a D for divorce on my chest. I had hit rock bottom.

Something clicked when I went through my divorce. It's hard to explain, but I will try. My parents talked to their Guru (spiritual teacher) about me because they were so worried about my future. One day, he told my parents to marry me off because that would change my life. I feel silly repeating this, but this is precisely what happened.

Getting married and divorced within the span of four months was like an out-of-body experience, but I needed it to wake me up out of my slumber. My divorce made me realize that I needed to like who I am and choose myself first.

Choosing to Serve

During that time, my brother mentioned something about counseling and psychology. He said, "Bena (sister in my native language), you have been through so much in your life. Because of that, you have this innate ability to understand other people's pain. You should maybe think about going into the counseling field." I had no idea what that meant because the only acceptable profession I was exposed to was the medical profession to follow in my parent's footsteps.

When my brother said counseling, something clicked. I listened! My grades were horrible, however. As mentioned, I had failed out of three colleges. I did have a college degree, but just barely. My dad, being the fixer he is, went to work to help me. My dad used his connections at the hospital he worked to get me into a master's program in community counseling on a conditional basis. So as my divorce was finalizing, I got my letter of conditional acceptance to Eastern Michigan University in their Counseling Department.

I have never cried so much in my life. It was tears of pain and utter gratefulness that, through my divorce, I could sense a purpose. I felt that there was a reason why my life was as confusing as it was. I would have never chosen the field I was about to embark on had I followed the expected path. The energy I felt is hard to describe. But, for the first time in my life, I felt hopeful because I had a goal that felt true to who I am.

Reflections on Suffering

Suffering and pain are a part of everyone's life. What helped me was being seen by my brother. He saw things in me that I could not because I was too busy comparing myself to a standard I could never meet. Because I felt unseen for most of my life, I never went on a journey to discover who I am. I never felt safe in my body to do that. I never thought I was worth the time to get to know. More importantly, I felt if someone else did not choose me, then I must not be worthy.

I chose men who were too busy for me, whether it was because of their work, interests, or friends. I chose this because it felt normal to me. After all, I was used to chasing attention from others. After the initial honeymoon period would wear off (the initial dopamine hit), I would feel like a burden because I would expect more. My insecurities would flare, and I would scream to feel seen and heard. That is when I would be told I was too much, and the relationship would end.

Reflections on Surrender

Failed relationships were the pattern I had known all too well. But, instead of pausing and reflecting on this pattern, I would blame the other person and start my search for the next man that I would swear would meet all my needs. It was not until my brother saw me after my divorce that I realized that I am the common denominator in the story of my life. I realized I could no longer blame the men I chose to date/marry, my culture, my parents, and the community I grew up in for my choices.

I realized that if I did not connect with my inherent worth, I would continue searching for it in all the wrong places. I won't say I feel 100% worthy of who I am; those inner child wounds still get triggered, but I am much more self-aware because I am doing the inner work needed to heal. I wanted to share my story because I genuinely believe in the power of feeling seen, heard, and accepted. It is at the core of what every human needs to fulfill their purpose in life. If I can do it, I hope it will inspire others to go on this journey of self-healing.

Welcoming Self-Healing

I am proud to share that I finished all the required schooling to become Dr. Paulomi Campbell, Ph.D. I am remarried, and I have two wonderful sons. Though on the outside, it looks like my life is together, I need to be honest because the title of my chapter is about authenticity. To honor that, I will say that my marriage is far from perfect. It continues to trigger many of the wounds that are still very much alive in me. The only change is that because I am committed to my inner work, I am learning to see my husband as my greatest teacher in life.

I am learning to see him as an assignment given to me by God because He loves me. I have the choice to see His assignment as an opportunity to strengthen my conviction to grow and learn about who I truly am. Or, I have the option to see His assignment through the lens of resentment, which deepens my fear and blocks me from love completely.

I have leaned heavily on my connection with God through my healing journey. I have learned that I can only access my spiritual power if I am honest with myself, remain disciplined with what my body, mind, and soul need to feel balanced, and practice self-acceptance. Therefore, I can see the assignment that, in my case, my husband as less of a problem but as an opportunity for me to strengthen my spiritual connection.

After the pandemic, I decided that my personal journey of healing could no longer be separated from how I work with my clients. This means that I no longer see mental health symptoms as problems that must be fixed. I also share my own story with my clients because I want them to know that I am just as human as they are. I am not the expert on their life; they are. I believe I am my client's guide showing them how to view their "symptoms" as messages from the body, mind, and soul telling them where they need to focus on healing. After all, it is only when we heal from our past that we can find our purpose.

At the core of my practice is believing in the good of every client, no matter what they are going through now or carrying from their past. This helps clients soften and take responsibility for the patterns that keep showing up in their lives. From this place, they can discover their core values and beliefs. I believe that when you know who you are, you will naturally know what is suitable for you; your boundaries will become clear.

This knowing includes knowing what foods work with your body, what thoughts/beliefs feel right to you, what movement is suitable for your body, etc. Once clients are clear on their core values/beliefs, they are encouraged to practice meeting their needs daily with loving support. Building positive habits is at the core of self-healing because it grounds us and makes us feel safe and loved. From my personal and professional experience, I know that living your most genuine life is possible if you are committed to doing the work.

"I have the choice to see His assignment as an opportunity to strengthen my conviction to grow and learn about who I truly am. Or I have the choice to see His assignment through the lens of resentment, which deepens my fear and blocks me from love completely."

Paulomi Campbell

About Paulomi Campbell

Paulomi Campbell was born In Mumbai, India, to two medical doctor parents who moved to Flint, Michigan, where she was raised. Her parents migrated to America to give their children more opportunities, such as a life with greater concerns than the day-to-day struggles and discomforts they faced growing up in India. Paulomi's journey did not lead her to what was expected (medical school). Instead, it led her to a Ph.D. in Counseling Psychology from SUNY Buffalo with a specialization in Health Psychology.

During her internship at the Atlanta VAMC and post-doctoral fellowship at Emory University, she worked with clients with chronic medical conditions such as cancer and HIV. She was technically in the medical field, but in a way that was more aligned with her strengths. Though she had the privilege of working in various medical settings, traditional psychotherapy left her wanting more for her patients and herself. During the pandemic, she discovered how she wanted to serve the clients that choose to work with her. This is how Inara Therapy + Wellness was born. Her passion lies in guiding clients back to themselves and healing the wounded parts so they can come back home to who they truly are.

Author/ Contact Information:
www.inaratherapy.com
hello@inaratherapy.com
704-946-5606
@inaratherapyandwellness

Chapter 4
Welcome Home, Jersey Girl!
Robin H. Clare

Growing up in New Jersey, I had a feisty side to my personality that I named Jersey Girl. She was a beautiful, badass chick that was super fun, and nobody messed with her. She was an influencer and held leadership positions in her school. She was funny and popular, unaware of how powerful she was. She manifested precisely what she desired until she switched careers and stopped manifesting, and life became increasingly frustrating.

To understand Jersey Girl, one must first get to know me. I grew up in a neighborhood where I was the only girl. This included my two brothers and all the boys I played football and army with. I went on all the boy adventures. I was a tomboy and continued to play football until it hurt to be tackled because at nine years old, I had my period and became "a woman," and my mom suggested I stop playing.

Maturing Too Fast

Even at nine years old, I became bewildered over my place in the world. Why couldn't I play with my guy friends? How do I make friends with girls? Why does everyone (boys, men, girls, women) look at me so funny? I had boobs and a shape, and I was the only girl with her period in fifth grade. My mom would watch my ever-maturing body and say on each birthday, "Thank goodness, she is 10....11....12....13....14.

Finally, the other girls began to catch up with me in late middle and high school. I missed playing with the boys and became sexually active much earlier than I was emotionally ready for. I became very popular and was voted president of my high school class twice and voted Miss Junior Class and Miss Senior Class. I did the bare minimum to get good grades and relied on my class officer positions to get into college.

During high school, I was part of a group of kids that got stoned all the time. I discovered that I could have the munchies, eat like a pig, and then throw up my food. This led to a 40-year addiction to obsessive-compulsive food disorder and bulimia. Bulimia became a form of self-humiliation to protect me from the humiliation I felt as a young woman and the reaction of others to my fully developed body.

Before the #MeToo Movement

I went off to college and experienced deep, passionate love. I had my heart shattered into many pieces by my college love due to an immaturity that led to cheating. I left college shaken and unsure of how to take myself into the real world. After graduating from college, I entered the workplace in a small public accounting firm. Two of the partners took a strong interest in me.

One of them would ask me to accompany him to lunch as a showpiece, and the other would sexually harass me by rubbing up against me while showing me how to do an accounting worksheet. This job lasted one year, and I was fired for embarrassing the more handsy partner by calling him out in front of the other partners. Because I was unsteady in my power, I was sexually harassed and then fired. This was before the "me too" movement and, frankly, just the way it was. But Jersey Girl was getting madder.

Entering the Masculine Corporate World

I picked myself up and went further in the corporate world with Jersey Girl in tow and was met with a blast of unprecedented masculine energy. This masculine energy of corporate America in the 1980s was ruthless, underhanded, and bold. How would Jersey Girl, in her proper badass way, shift to accommodate this new level of competitive energy in corporate America? She would adapt, and she would become successful.

She would use her beauty, brains, and feminine energy to get what she wanted. She would learn to become underhanded and shift blame. She would learn to "play with the men"—as she played with the boys in her neighborhood. In the 1980s, women had to beat men at their own game at work and be twice as tough to get ahead. Jersey Girl was in charge of my corporate life

For example, my first husband and I worked at a bank in downtown Hartford. One of the salespeople he worked with was trying to steal him from me. As an expense accountant, I audited her and got her in trouble for improper expense padding of her reimbursement account. This was the first time Jersey Girl came to work with me.

Jersey Girl would continue to influence me, this time in my personal life. In a divorce conversation with my first husband, he thought he deserved more than me in the settlement because he made more money than me. I fought for my rightful half of our assets. He was shocked because he had no idea I had that level of tenacity. Perhaps I even shocked myself!

Finding My Way After Divorce

After our divorce, I began a 20-year career at a major insurance company, but this also started a period of dating anyone interesting, partying, and having fun. Unfortunately, because of many nights out during the work week, I began to fail at my job, but a supervisor asked if I wanted her to retrain me to get me back on track. I am forever grateful to this co-worker who saw my value. After that, I decided to get serious about my career and manifested ten promotions in 20 years.

During this time, I met a man who wanted to marry me, and I wasn't sure. He and I went to Las Vegas to visit my brother, who worked in the casino business. I prayed to God for a sign that I should marry him. My brother brought us to a casino and agreed to split the money three ways if any of us won. He won $258,000 on a progressive slot machine.

Sure, that was a good sign, but he decided he did not want to share the money since he had been poor his whole life. I convinced him to give my brother a monetary gift. After all, he would not have been in Las Vegas without my brother. Ultimately, I realized he was not a man of his word, and I broke up with him. He could not believe I would break up with him after he was "rich," but Jersey Girl stood firm about needing a man of integrity. Until then, I did not realize how vital the standard of integrity was in my life.

Jersey Girl was present in my successful career in corporate America, ensuring that I had all the same opportunities as the men and fighting for equal pay for an equal position. While I loved her, she was not always well-received in the workplace; she was considered aggressive and not assertive like her male counterparts. Nevertheless, I was part of an army of working women who thought we could have it all.

Jersey Girl at Home

Soon after, I met my man of integrity, my current husband, and the father of my children. I knew right away that he was my true earth mate, we are both powerful and loving, and yet, he, like no other, can bring out Jersey Girl's feisty nature. When I looked up the definition of Jersey Girl in the Urban Dictionary, I read,

"Almost always a lady until you mess with her, and then she will kick your butt. But she is the best kind of friend and mother."

Jersey Girl was always welcome at home; my husband loved my tenacious caregiving of our family and my ability to stand on my own two feet. He loved my being the working mom—making a living while raising our two children. About 17 years into my last full-time job, I began to hear the calling to live and work more spiritually. Unfortunately, this spiritual lifestyle was incompatible with the corporate environment. I had to leave my cushy job to follow my spiritual path to a career in the healing arts.

Jersey Girl Became Burnt Out

My spiritual mantra became "Bring it On," I studied with spiritual masters and began healing my traumatic past. Jersey Girl added a level of tenacity to my spiritual path, but she unconsciously decided to take a break from the business side of making money. To be honest, I was tired of Jersey Girl's aggressive masculine; therefore, I withheld my masculine, and my business suffered.

In my frustration, I blamed others for my lack of success and continued to punish myself through overeating and bulimia. I also began a deep study of the Law of Attraction. I even organized four events a year over 12 years for the spiritual community to share the teaching of Abraham Hicks—a leading voice in abundance. Then, one day, I received a message from a spirit guide, "Even though you are an expert in the Law of Attraction, you really suck at it." I was unclear about what was missing from my formula for success.

Jersey Girl and the Spiritual Path

If we defined Jersey Girl from a spiritual perspective, I would describe her as the masculine energy of my Soul. My feminine energy was creating a spiritual business, but I was failing in manifesting abundance in the business. Our masculine energy only responds to us when we uphold our feminine energy standards with impeccable integrity. Therefore, I would never make money in my business until I welcomed back Jersey Girl (i.e., my masculine energy).

For many years in my spiritual career, I went overboard in the feminine, believing that going with the flow and partnering with Spirit would make me successful. Unfortunately, what was missing was my masculine energy of relentless pursuit of my goals. I needed to take whatever action needed and not excuse a lack of profit as a message from Spirit to shift gears. The bottom line, I had to become accountable for my success.

This meant becoming the perfect integration of my high feminine (creativity and compassion) and my high masculine (action and abundance). This also meant I needed to hold exacting standards with impeccable integrity in my personal and professional life, stop blaming others for my lack of abundance, and, most importantly, be clear on what truly matters to me in my life. Only then could I manifest the life I most desire.

Jersey Girl Returns

Jersey Girl returned with a vengeance when my 95-year-old mother began her decline, and the end of her life was drawing near. I was busy trying to manage family personalities and the care from Assisted Living and hospice, and it became apparent to Jersey Girl that my mother was receiving conflicting care.

I remember the exact moment Jersey Girl returned. I was standing outside taking a stress break at the Assisted Living facility, when Jersey Girl declared, "I am taking over your mother's care; enough with spiritual Robin, she is being ineffective."

Once again, I became tenacious and tough but fair and developed the authority most needed for my mom's care. It was difficult because my stepdad was in denial, and my mom was dying. Meanwhile, spiritual Robin was watching Jersey Girl and liking this version of herself.

I began to ask myself how I could bring back Jersey Girl without being aggressive and snarky. Because I have always been Jersey Girl, but perhaps I didn't like the version of her that I knew before in my corporate days.

Honoring Your Jersey Girl

As you read this chapter, I hope you can recognize the Jersey Girl or Guy in yourself. The tough, tenacious "get it done" aspect of your life. I am confident that there is room for assertiveness and abundance on the spiritual path. However, for many spiritual business people, it takes an effort to move beyond the vow of poverty that is the perception in our community.

To have a successful life, I invite you to see where you are not honoring yourself or not creating a lifestyle of abundance and find out why. Unfortunately, we often blame others for our lack of follow-through and use their negativity to influence our outcomes.

How would your life be different if you lived in the flow of life, released your inner conflicts, held yourself accountable, and did not enable others to sabotage your dreams?

Here are the changes you would quickly begin to notice in your life, you would:

1. Value yourself deeply and apply that in all parts of your life.

2. Be in a relationship with only others who support your vision.

3. Speak your truth in both your personal and professional lives.

4. Seek the answers to your life from within, not Spirit or others.

5. Trust your intuition, wisdom, and genius.

6. Figure out what truly matters to you and manifest it.

Becoming the Divine Warrior

Today, Jersey Girl is not aggressive but a confident combination of assertiveness, action, and attraction. My integrated feminine and masculine self has correlated to a more peaceful environment at home, growth in financial abundance in my business, and higher standards in all parts of my life. I am now in long-term recovery from food addictions, and I honor Jersey Girl—the Divine Warrior who is here to be of service to her family, the world, and herself.

"I now know that when I hold exacting standards with impeccable integrity in my personal and professional life and I am clear on what truly matters to me in my life, I will manifest the life I most desire."
Robin H. Clare

About Robin H. Clare

Robin H. Clare's path to fulfilling her destiny began by leaving her traditional 25-year MBA business career and traveling the globe to study with spiritual masters. But, first, Robin had to reveal her deep secret of struggling for four decades with food addiction and bulimia. Now in grounded recovery, Robin is an award-winning coach, recovery medium, best-selling spiritual author, and highly regarded speaker and teacher. In addition, she is a writing coach and manuscript maven for Green Heart Living Press.

She has documented her extraordinary spiritual journey in the highly-acclaimed *Messiah Within*, followed by Amazon bestsellers, *The Divine Keys*, and *Feast & Famine*. In 2021, she released an ebook and recorded divine meditations in *King Solomon Speaks*. She will release *The Hidden Truth Within Trauma* in 2023. Awards include 10 Best Life/Business Coaches and 10 Best Energy Healers in the Natural Nutmeg Readers Polls of 2017-2022. Certifications include Recovery Coach Professional™, Advanced Akashic Record reader, Reiki Master, 13th Octave LaHoChi practitioner, and National Speakers Academy certified keynote speaker. Robin is a channel for the Ascended Masters.

Author Contact Information:
https://clare-ity.squarespace.com
IG: @clareitybyrobin
FB: @clareitywithrobin

Chapter 5

Depression as a Spiritual Path

Mary Constance

Depression happens when you cannot connect, trust, or believe in yourself and your true nature. You may not connect the two for many years, or for most of this lifetime, like myself. For years, I wanted freedom from the relentless fear and depression that took over my life from early adulthood. I now know that I incarnated this lifetime to see that my depression is a guide and a spiritual path to learning my true nature.

Early Identity Formation

As a young child, I lost my voice and ability to express myself. As a toddler, I was separated from my parents due to an illness that created anxiety, fear, and aloneness. Also, my teacher reprimanded me for talking during a kindergarten class, banished me from the classroom, and isolated me for that behavior. These early trauma experiences contributed to the silence I experienced and my need to internalize my thoughts and feelings.

My initial quietness as a young child didn't fit what society and my family expected of me. Therefore, as I received criticism and teasing as a young child, I became more fearful and believed something was wrong with my quietness. As a result, I became content to play quietly and alone at times. Yet, playing with friends as a very young child was necessary for self-expression, movement, and laughter.

In her book, *Quiet*, Susan Cain[1] encourages parents to not label a child as *"shy"* as it may contribute to the child believing that *shyness* or *quietness* is negative and bad. "She'll believe the label and experience her nervousness as a fixed trait rather than an emotion she can control. Above all, do not shame her for her *shyness*".

The programs and beliefs instilled in our society that you are not contributing if you don't speak up can be excruciatingly painful. In the classroom, I was less able to think about what I could say until I left the classroom. It was then too late to say what surfaced in my mind about the topic/discussion. I would be viewed as not intelligent because of my quietness.

To some, my quietness was viewed as being fearful and simple, and to others as trying to gain attention. My nickname in high school was "Mum's the Word," by I am sure unconscious but well-meaning friends, primarily males. I would laugh this off as many were my friends, and it was some gesture to try and connect with me. Unfortunately, the nickname only exacerbated my fear and lack of belonging and being accepted.

Through the years, my ability to express myself improved slowly. However, I always felt that wave of fear. The insecurity about speaking up and fear of being seen as stupid and incompetent plagued me for most of my adult life. I would avoid situations or gatherings to avoid being seen as less intelligent, for speaking up was difficult. I would try to hide, hoping not to be seen as quiet, but the more I tried to hide within a group, the more I was seen.

My ability to trust my thoughts and feelings dwindled, and I became self-critical, hiding more and praying to learn to speak up. This lack of self-esteem evolved into a major depression in my early twenties which is when I chose, through a suggestion by an

---

[1] Cain, Susan. Quiet, *The Power of Introverts in a World that Can't Stop Talking*. Crown, 2013.

older brother, to enter therapy.

I thought my life mission was to belong and fit in with society's expectations. I did not know who I was or why I was here. During the depressive periods, I prayed to return to someplace safe without the pressure to speak and belong, a place that felt more like home where I could be accepted for who I was.

The pressure to speak up is great in our society. There is pressure in our school systems and work environments. With this pressure to speak growing for me through the years, I lost my attention, voice, and memory, never feeling OK with just being and taking in information as that was my particular way of learning.

Exploration Through An Examined Life

Most of my early experiences in therapy were focused on learning how, why, and where I lost my voice and the ability to express myself. I was determined to fit in with my peers and society. This examined life also led me to begin my spiritual path. However, I continued to struggle with depression.

I fit in through finding a pseudo-self yet never really found my authentic voice. Silence and observing took over my many group encounters. Yet, competition and the need to be something important took precedence. I would have to be perfect and be something special to belong and feel worthy.

Part of my spiritual path was learning to BE present in the moment. However, my ego wanted me to "Be Something"—to be something important. "Be seen. Speak up." Those programs and desires haunted me much of my life as I never felt I could reach them. Eckhart Tolle refers to the challenge in life as having the willfulness of being able to feel worthy within oneself, without needing to be important, but to be present in the moment and simply "ordinary."

Journey Through Hope to Awareness

Living an examined life gave me *hope* and allowed me to step back and see the larger picture and change the lens through which I viewed my life. You and I are not broken. You already have a sense of wholeness within you of the *divine essence* to which you truly want to aspire. If your history truly defined you, you would not be curious, questioning, experiencing deep feelings, or seeking help. Having an *awareness* of essence prevents you from having to live the personality self or ego.

Each step of *hope* in your life leads to a step of greater *hope*, a step of greater promise...and then another step of *hope* leading you to the clarity of expression of Spirit. Each step of *hope* gives you a roadmap to follow. At some point, *hope* becomes *awareness*. When one realizes that *hope* leads to *awareness*, there is a knowing inside you versus trusting the external messages and programs.

Unveiling of the Mission

I have learned through therapy and being on the spiritual path that I incarnated to experience, as a very young child, what it would be like to be quiet, simple, and contemplative and to journey through the trials and tribulations of finally choosing this lifestyle as an adult. I have discovered that the thirty years of on and off depression was a catalyst for fulfilling my mission. I wore my depression like a comforting blanket most of my life, thus hiding from my true nature and purpose in this incarnation.

As I write my story, I hear a firm, strong inner voice telling me; you get this. You knew this well before you arrived on this planet. This is why you are here. Tell your story. It is already inside you. Reveal your truth. The time is now! People need to hear this. It will help them to discover their truth, unlock, and discover their wisdom as you are doing now as you put these words to paper.

Realization of the Inner Monk

The time of COVID was both extremely hard and transformative for me. The aloneness and loneliness reawakened my depression that lay dormant for several years as I pursued my spiritual path. I was beginning to understand this lifelong depression. Having this quiet time to slow down and reflect is where I learned about my true nature and how being quiet, contemplative, and simple were all part of my mission and divine plan. I was more at arm's length from my depression.

Depression was my identity. I had not yet been able to embrace and accept depression as a spiritual path. I call this being at the *threshold of depression*. Being at arm's length means the time is not right yet to leap into awareness of my true purpose and true nature. Something kept me from embracing the aloneness and wrapping myself in its safety rather than in fear.

Over many years of reflection on my spiritual path, I encountered a past life memory that explained why I chose to experience periods of aloneness in my life. The regression exercise surfaced because I experienced a devastating loss in a past lifetime and took my own life. I believed I failed as a human being, yet I was a hero. Therefore, I chose to incarnate this life to heal that lifetime and realize my bravery and courage through re-experiencing the feelings of depression and aloneness and clearing the old karma.

Yet, I also realized that my true mission was to honor myself as an empathic soul—one who helps anchor and hold the Light for our planet. Some of the attributes of the empathic soul align with my true nature. These qualities, sensitivity, intuition, and heart-centeredness are essential in anchoring and holding the Light. I am here to fulfill the empathic soul contract I made before incarnating on this planet. All the qualities of an empathic soul match what I have identified as attributes of my Inner Monk.

Attributes of the Inner Monk

Like many of us, I chose to live this life of depression to discover my true nature. Even with their depression, many lightworkers are helping and assisting humanity in this phase of the planet's evolution. I now invite you to review the attributes of your Inner Monk and see if they resonate with you. It's time to know that you do not need to conform to society but follow your unique soul path to serve others.

Simple: Living a basic life and foregoing a lavish lifestyle defined by our culture.

Quiet: Knowing that not speaking is a form of reflection and inner confidence.

Contemplative: Sitting in silence and not needing to share your perspective with others.

Stillness: Eliminating the noise and chatter of the outside world and finding safety and peace in solitude.

Non-Traditional: Accepting a path that does not conform to society's values.

Seeking the Truth: Searching for meaning that aligns with your heart and soul.

Commitment: Creating and living an examined life that supports your emotional, physical, and spiritual growth.

Empathic: Recognizing your sensitive nature is a gift to others you encounter on your journey.

From the Threshold to True Nature

What will you find when you live in your true nature? I

discovered a life with more peace and *hope*. Moving beyond the *threshold of depression* takes a leap of faith and loving yourself unconditionally. It requires you to continue to reflect, unfold and embrace increased consciousness and presence. Living your true nature will enable you to know your Divine Essence. I invite you to see this time on earth as a training ground to realize your true nature and to explore and remember who you truly are.

You will have to embrace your aloneness and loneliness to accomplish this leap. You may feel moments of *hope* from depression dissolve into disappointment and fear once again—for, after all, it is a cycle. However, you will become the observer of your life instead of desiring to leave this planet in frustration. You will honor both the ups and the downs. Going home is the return to your true nature, which is self-love and self-acceptance.

From Depression to Ascension

I am sharing a message from my soul about my depression and feelings of this paralyzing aloneness during COVID. "Breath into the feelings. They are not all yours; you are here to help clear the collective aloneness by healing yourself. You have been doing that your entire life." Elizabeth Wood, a seer and scientist, speaks about this time of the Ascension of our planet as an opportunity to bring Light to the fears created by these early traumas and traumas from other lifetimes.

In the past, there was a tendency, and it was acceptable to try to "get rid of depression," thinking it was wrong. Intuitive strategist and spiritual teacher, Robert Ohotto, describes the empathic individual as highly sensitive and intuitive and that they cannot always identify why they may feel depressed, alone, and fearful. Now, in this time of Ascension, we need to feel everything to be able to alchemize our feelings into Light and assist in planet earth's evolution. I was reminded of the significant changes taking place in the transformation and evolution of our planet into unity consciousness

Whatever you feel, whether depression, anxiety, grief, or anger, let these feelings remind you that you are on the right track to your healing. There is absolutely nothing wrong with you for having these human emotions. These feelings, whether lifelong depression or any other, are not who we truly are. I am not my depression, sadness, grief, or anger; neither are you.

From Hope to Awareness to Certainty

Hope to *awareness* to *certainty* is where you declare who you are and your expression on earth. Transformation happens when you accept *awareness* to *certainty.* But, first, your mind has to accept that all these things happened with good purpose, including depression. In Sacred Alchemy (a spiritual healing technique), you learn not to make the depression go away but to accept, feel it through completely, have compassion for the entire process, and let it flow through and pass.

Emotions are nothing more than "energy in motion moving through you." Ultimately, you will gain an understanding and *awareness* of your depression and proceed on the road *to certainty*, seeing the truth and accepting your depression as the path. Living an examined life was always the *hope* of finding the truth. This *certainty* is the trust in the Sacred Alchemy and depression as a way to reach that truth at each level of our ever-unfolding life.

Depression as a Spiritual Path

The attributes of the Inner Monk and being non-traditional is something I fought for and perhaps did not know why. My Inner Monk had its qualities, priorities, and ways of being in the world, and I fought for that. When I could not fight for my Inner Monk attributes, I suffered for years in and out of depression. When I couldn't stay in the power of the Inner Monk, then the depression was the only way of coping with societal norms I knew were not correct for me. Depression was a protection and a way of taking the pressure off.

I now honor that my true nature has the qualities of the Inner Monk, all of which I was familiar with but also denied. I was looking for my spiritual voice all along but did not know this. I, therefore, tried to find the voice that would help me fit into society and belong. By honoring my Inner Monk, I recognize my most significant attributes while knowing I have always belonged to the greater whole of humanity in Oneness.

"Whatever you feel, whether depression, anxiety, grief, or anger, let these feelings remind you that you are on the right track to your healing. There is absolutely nothing wrong with you for having these human emotions."

Mary Constance

About Mary Constance

Mary Constance Lombardo, LCSW, has been a Licensed Psychotherapist for over 30 years and is in private practice at the Bridge Healing Arts Center in Farmington, Connecticut. While engaged on her spiritual journey over the last 30 years, she has studied various modalities including Buddhism with an emphasis on psycho-spiritual development and healing.

Author Contact Information:
https://bridgehac.com
M-Lombardo@sbcglobal.net

Chapter 6

Discovering the Truth About Jesus and Myself

Holly Dudash

Jesus Christ. Yes, Him. Who is this man? Is He God or just a historical figure? This is the question I have been asking myself since I was sitting in the church pews of my Catholic church as a young girl. I only attended "adult church," so I would sit on the wooden bench and follow my mother's lead to open the Bible to a certain page, get on our knees to pray, and turn to our neighbors and wish them, "Peace be with you."

Jesus was as unknown to me at home as He was in church. I did not understand the priest, and I really could not relate to the fire and brimstone teachings that led me to believe I was a sinner and I would burn in hell forever upon death. This certainly was not the Jesus I wanted to follow. Perhaps if I had attended "children's church," Jesus would have been a cartoon character full of love, fun, and games. Maybe I would have grown up to adore Him because I learned about Him from the viewpoint of a child instead of an adult.

No wonder I spent the next decades searching for the real Jesus. Not in Christianity, but in the exploration of pop culture, of studying world religions in school, and in taking on the religious identities of Agnostic, Wiccan, Spiritual but not religious, and None, all before converting to evangelical Christianity.

I am grateful to have already lived a life of incredible and memorable experiences full of travel, and time spent with family and friends. I chose to follow my heart and pursue my dreams, making good choices along the way. Sometimes they were with a significant other, but many times they were accomplished by myself. These were my hopes and dreams, and as I set my heart on them, I did the hard work to make them come true.

Being a lifelong learner makes it easy to be curious about myself and about the world we live in, as well as the amazing opportunities there are to explore, discover, and live the life of your dreams! Although I grew up in a secular household, attended public schools, excelled academically, played high school sports, worked part-time, and graduated college before studying abroad twice in France, there was something missing from the richness of my life. I still did not know who Jesus was, and I longed to find out why so many people believed in Him. Why did I celebrate Christmas and Easter the secular way when I had an underlying desire to *know* Him?

I Followed My Intuition Right Into Church!

That all began to change in my late 30s when the Holy Spirit moved so deeply within me that I simply had to do what it was whispering to me daily. I had to go to church, and I did. That first Sunday morning bright and early for the 8:00 a.m. service, I was anxious upon entering those Christian church doors. By the time I left, I had already made new friends, and I knew what my next steps were to learn about Jesus and His friends.

I continued going to church on Sundays, but Christianity soon became a daily event in my new religious life. My initial impressions of my contemporary church were that it was like a liberal arts college where you got to pick and choose your "courses." Yes, you could study the Holy Bible in Bible 101 or make it more informal as a discussion in the homes of church members. You could volunteer your time, money, and resources in endless ways. You could also take extracurricular activities according to your interests such as culinary arts, chorus, theater, finance, women's and men's studies, study abroad, etc. You could work in administration, or with children, teens, or young adults. There was always an upcoming activity open to the secular public that provided ample opportunity to develop new skills, meet new people, and spread the love of Jesus.

Admittedly, I had an idyllic transition to religion as a mature adult. I immediately found the right church for me that was welcoming, and it enabled me to fit in and participate as much or as little as I wanted. They gave me Bibles and they gave me the Biblical teachings I craved, as well as fellowship, friendships, prayer, communion, meals, and the very best day of my life when I was baptized in the name of God the Father, Jesus the Son, and the Holy Spirit. I was over the moon with joy and praise for God. Now, this Jesus is the Jesus I could worship for the rest of my life!

My relationship with Jesus was solid. I had read the Bible in a record six months, so I quickly came up to speed with the Biblical stories that our pastors would share along with a modern reference point that would tie history with the present to show us how to love like Jesus. We did not just worship Jesus as our God in heaven, we followed Jesus, as we shed the unhealthy, sinful, secular ways of living for ourselves, and we adopted a healthy, truly Christian life. My life was completely changed by the way I believed, acted, loved, and carried myself. I was doing God's work every single day, praising Him, and doing so much good for others in His name. I could not imagine what would soon happen to me by the first Easter after my baptism, which caused me immense pain and trauma.

Holy Week Drama

As I was preparing myself for Holy Week, I was learning

about the events that occurred to Lord Jesus leading up to the cross. I read about them, and as I began processing them, I was overwhelmed with compassion for Him and all that He suffered for us. However, what I thought were normal emotions felt by most Christians for Lord Jesus were nothing compared to the trauma response for me that got worse leading up to Easter. I realized my Christian friends were not experiencing this devastating reaction, and I knew I needed more information to explain my own suffering so I could begin healing myself.

The answers could not be found in the church or in the Bible. Even praying to Lord Jesus was unsatisfactory, so by default, I chose to seek out answers from the spiritual and psychic communities. My session for an Akashic Records reading was eye-opening, to say the least. The Akashic Records are your personal vault of every lifetime, every thought, and every experience that your soul has ever had. The gifted psychic revealed my soul's truth that I was a Roman soldier who had witnessed the events of Holy Week, and the torture and trials that Jesus experienced in his final days through His world-changing crucifixion.

I was grateful to learn I felt love and compassion towards Jesus in those moments of pain, humiliation, suffering, and in taking His last breath. However, I had to remain stoic in my position, and I never got to process the effect of witnessing this horror which taught me compassion for humanity. My soul remembers and the time to heal is now.

Spiritual Healing is a Blessing

I intuitively knew that I needed to keep working with psychic mediums who used various modalities to help me learn more about myself, and who I really am as a divine being of light. Even though I know what the Biblical scriptures say about seeking out psychics, I could not heal myself by going to church on Sundays and reading my Bible or praying. Those are the methods used when you choose to stay on the religious path. They can be as effective as you make them out to be. However, my consciousness was expanding, and I knew to listen to my intuition and follow the calling of my sacred heart by transitioning to the spiritual path. This is the path that Jesus the Christ actually followed when He walked the Earth 2,000 years ago. It is also the path that I am called to teach you today.

As an evangelical Christian, I was a true believer in taking the Bible as the literal inspired Word of God with all its contradictions, hatred, and suffering because anything is possible with God, right? Therefore, it was highly unlikely that I would embrace the spiritual path. However, I was soon delighted by how amazing I felt after a sound healing session with crystals, singing bowls, and divine guidance. I always left in a truly blissful state that was unmatched by Christianity because the healing I experienced was on another level; inter-dimensional, multi-dimensional, and always sensational!

Journaling in my Christian women's journal used to be my way of connecting with God through writing. After doing the inner work to heal myself, I would journal about spiritual things, and the greater my healing, the more spiritual gifts would be revealed. The gift of automatic writing was both a surprise and a delight to me, as the unique experience of literally being guided to write by the divine is a wonder in itself. The divine messages are truly magical, and they taught me who I really am as a spiritual being on a mission to raise awareness of Jesus' genuine teachings, to heal my mind, body, soul, and spirit, and to bring Christ Consciousness with every step I take on Earth.

Writing Heals and Releasing Trauma Brings You Peace

I also began learning about my soul's purpose which involves more writing to bring the messages of Jesus the Christ to the modern world. I joined a popular writer's community, hired a gifted writing coach, and I began writing chapter after chapter for my debut literary work about my spiritual awakening, and the teachings of Jesus. I meditated and I listened to 432 Hz or 528 Hz healing music each time I sat down to write, and it worked as I was left in a state of peace, tranquility, and calm. My writing is divinely inspired and is better than if I had chosen to write without this healing music.

I researched my subject matter extensively, and I learned more about spirituality. This took me farther away from evangelical Christianity as I embraced metaphysics, contemplative Christianity, and mysticism. I love being a student so I enrolled in an online program to become an accredited, certified Spiritual Psychology Coach and a Spiritual Psychology Master Practitioner. I chose a particular program that allows you to heal from your own trauma using the proprietary E4 Trauma Method®. I can personally attest to experiencing and witnessing the fast and effective method to heal your trauma by reprogramming your subconscious mind and creating wonderful new declarations for yourself.

You Are Not Alone As You Spiritually Awaken

If my surrender story resonates with you, and if you are experiencing something similar, there are many things you can do. Begin by getting curious and asking questions. Maybe you notice something is not quite right about your religious path, and you are ready to follow your soul's calling on the spiritual path. You'll need to start reading and learning everything you can about the great awakening that is occurring to human beings during this cyclical opportunity for soul growth and ascension into higher dimensions.

Spiritual awakenings are not for the faint of heart. You will become a truth seeker as you put the pieces of the infinite cosmic puzzle together. Esoteric knowledge and spiritual truths will open your mind to the nature of our reality, the universe, and the one Source of creation that connects us as One. You will learn the role of religion throughout the ages, and the political partnerships that have been used to restrain human beings for millennia from reaching their highest potential as they remember who they really are as individualized expressions of this creator Source. You will learn about your spiritual gifts, Universal Law, and why our situation on Earth is the way it is. Trust that everything is used for soul growth back to its origin. Trust also that some teachings, tools, and knowledge will intuitively feel right, while others will feel out of alignment with your truth. Follow this inner knowing.

Learning from others who have been down the spiritual path is a highly effective and recommended way to successfully navigate your spiritual awakening. Many experienced coaches and professionals in the spiritual community offer a plethora of modalities to help you learn what you need to at any given moment along your journey. It is very helpful to create a quiet, sacred space in your home where you can retreat regularly to begin praying, meditating, and simply getting quiet enough to hear your intuition, your spirit guides, and nature whispering their wisdom to you.

As you learn more about the influence of Universal Law and the creative process, you will begin to deeply visualize what it is you want to create for yourself in the form of manifesting your greatest desires. This takes dedication and guidance but is extremely rewarding. Universal Law and Spiritual Truth will teach you how you are the creator of your life with every experience pre-selected before you incarnated as your avatar on the surface of Earth, or selected by your ability to express yourself using free will and choice.

Loving, Caring Support is Available to You

Due to the unique conditions society has on Earth, including the illusion of duality and separation, every human experiences trauma in some form relative to them. Many of you may have received support from mental health professionals, and perhaps you have successfully resolved your traumas. I commend you for doing that as I have also worked with professionals around trauma.

Spiritual awakenings are unusual because they involve opening up to the reality of traumas not just from this lifetime, but from past lifetimes as well as generational and ancestral lineage traumas that were passed down the line of your ancestors to you, with the hopes that you will do the inner work necessary to end that particular trauma for generations back and yet to come.

If you can find a trained spiritual psychologist or psychology coach who understands this, they can help you navigate these traumas. Past-life regression, various forms of hypnotherapy, as well as the E4 Trauma Method® that I personally use to heal myself and others with, are some suggestions you should consider on your journey to heal yourself from the traumas of life on Earth throughout the ages and today.

If you enjoy reading and writing, you may find that writing can be very cathartic in helping you heal. You can simply begin writing on a piece of paper, typing your story, blogging online, or following the guidance of answering questions to help you understand yourself better as you continue on the spiritual path to awakening to your truth.

The spiritual community is full of loving souls who are

heart-centered, who already love and adore you as we know that all are One in the divine. This is the most incredible journey of your entire life, so where shall you begin?

With love, and light. Namaste! ♥

"However, my consciousness was expanding, and I knew to listen to my intuition and follow the calling of my sacred heart by transitioning to the spiritual path. This is the path that Jesus the Christ actually followed when He walked the Earth 2,000 years ago. It is also the path that I am called to teach you today."

Holly Dudash

About Holly Dudash

Holly Dudash is a lifelong learner, Maine-based published writer, founding member of the KSMG app, and spiritual teacher who experienced an incredible transformation during her spiritual awakening from being a devoted evangelical Christian to becoming a metaphysical Christian mystic. Holly follows her divine path as an accredited and certified Spiritual Psychology Coach and Master Practitioner through New Thought Global, and as a certified Wellness Counselor through Cornell University's eCornell.

Holly is passionate about educating others as a gifted storyteller and teacher, and she compassionately helps questioning Christians make the leap of faith to the spiritual path. As a French-trained esthetician, Holly creates sacred rituals to make spiritual practices meaningful, life-changing, and rewarding. Holly specializes in Spiritual Psychology for Christians, spiritual awakening, spiritual wellness and beauty, Christ Consciousness, soul ascension, Universal Law, and New Thought wisdom to co-create the 5th dimensional New Earth.

Contact Information:
Email: holly.dudash@protonmail.com

Chapter 7

Silence! Little Voice

Lowri Foyle

It's 1:00 and I'm in the yoga studio of the Recovery Center for Women's Living Sober class. At 12:55 every day we trudge up the stairs to the yoga room, take off our shoes, throw bolsters on the floor along the periphery of the room and sit on them. Some of the women make little couches with two or three bolsters which can be a problem because then there aren't enough for the stragglers to use. The older ladies pull up folding chairs to sit on because they can't get up from the floor once they're down there. The room always has the slight smell of stinky feet since it's August, really hot, and no one is wearing socks.

Today is Friday, otherwise known as 'Music Friday.' Lucky us! Sidney, the teacher, comes in holding a blaring speaker and dancing around like she's in an Abba video—arms outstretched—going round and round in circles. All twenty of us look at each other and roll our eyes. She runs in front of us and grabs at the hands of the women as she circles the room. I always feel nervous at this point because there's no way in hell I'm getting up and dancing with her. Thankfully, one reluctant person gets up and half-heartedly joins her dance for a minute or two.

Once Sidney finally gives up on the dance party she sits down on her bolster in the front. "Let's begin with a circle of friends," she says, "I'll start! Sidney, addict." We go around the room saying our names followed by either "alcoholic" or "addict." Some women say "alcoholic, addict," and the new woman says "both," which is really not allowed. Since it is Music Friday, Sidney asks one of the women to pick a song to play and explain to the group what its significance is to her. She goes around the circle asking various women to do the same thing.

When Sidney gets to me, I ask her to play *Wonderful Tonight* by Eric Clapton. Feeling pretty unsure of myself, I begin speaking... "Yesterday in the mail I received a photo album from my cousin Carol (she's crafty and sentimental like that). It was filled with pages of photos of my children over the years from Christmas cards I'd sent. As I looked longingly at each picture, I tried to imagine what I, the photographer, had looked like when they were two and four, six and eight... I thought about how much I loved my kids and how much I missed them, about how terrible it feels to be away from them."

Continuing, I said, "I used to be a good mother. I was always there to nurture and care for them, make them nice meals, read bedtime stories, and tuck them in every night. I used to get dressed up, do my hair and makeup, and go out to dinner or parties with my husband."

Suddenly, Susan across the circle bursts into tears and needs a tissue, so I stop talking. Kristy gets up with her bag and walks out of the room. Not sure what to do, I keep sharing because this is the most important part. "I want to be that person again. I'm not sure when I stopped doing those things, but it's like something just broke inside of me and I couldn't be her anymore."

I pause for a few seconds—a new thought enters my mind— so I say it. "But lately, being here at the Recovery Center, I've begun to feel a little kernel of light growing inside of me. It's saying, *go get 'em, you can do it.* The song is significant because I want to get back to the person I used to be. I want that light to keep growing brighter until my husband and children can tell me that I'm once again 'Wonderful Tonight.'"

The whole circle of women begins to clap. I guess some of them must feel the same way. I didn't realize I felt that way until I said the words out loud. Sidney plays the Clapton song. Some people sing along, some close their eyes, and some sniffle a little as they sway back and forth until the song ends.

It's 1:50. Living Sober is over now. We stand up, put away the bolsters, slip our shoes back on, and silently walk back down the stairs.

If I'm Sober, I'm Enough

I wrote that story the last time I went to rehab. It was the most wonderful, awful experience of my life. How completely baffling it was that in a fifty-minute group session in a yoga room, I could uncover feelings that I had stuffed way down inside myself for years, and then just go on with my day as if enlightenment into my soul was a regular occurrence. Yes, I had lost myself to alcohol, but I was determined to find myself again.

This is how my journey of recovery has unfolded—peeled like an onion—with layer upon layer of sadness, loss, fear, and anger that I finally began to feel once I stopped numbing myself with alcohol. I knew that this was it—I was going to get and stay sober—and have to face all those feelings I wanted to run and hide from. Not only did I stay for 30 days at rehab, but I went to sober living for three months afterward, just to be sure. I had been trying to get sober for five years and wasn't taking any chances this time.

Some of us have a little voice in our head that tells us we're not enough. Why wouldn't we listen to it? It's our own mind telling us. That voice was making me sick. I couldn't get better until I decided to stop listening to the voice that told me I was unworthy, not good enough, undeserving of love and goodness in my life. Since I was a perfectionist, I couldn't even acknowledge my natural gifts. Today, the sober me makes lists of my talents so I can remind myself that if I'm sober, I'm enough.

What I Used to Be Like

My story of addiction began about ten years ago. I had always liked to "party" with friends and family, but around 2012 it became an addiction. My son and I had moved to South Carolina so that he could attend golf school. My husband had stayed in Connecticut to take care of my daughter, who at the time was in boarding school. I was in a strange town and didn't know anyone. I felt sorry for myself. I was alone and suffered from the absence of my husband and daughter who were back in Connecticut. I didn't like our rental home and missed living in my beautiful house back in Connecticut. I missed my friends, family, and my old life.

Besides keeping busy with my son's golf tournaments and practices, I had too much free time during the day. One lucky day I wandered into a yoga studio and it became my new life's passion. I honestly think that yoga saved my life over those five years in Hilton Head. The problem was, other than yoga and reading books on spirituality, I had no life. I didn't want to go out at night with my single friends to bars and I was the third wheel at dinner with my married friends, so I stayed home every night drinking lots of wine. I'm not saying I had a glass of wine. When wine-o-clock hit, I would make dinner and drink a bottle of wine.

A very toxic pattern emerged where my son would come home from his exhausting day, eat dinner, then go into his room and shut the door while I tidied up and stayed in the living room. We didn't spend enough time together. I should have knocked on the door and gone in; he told me later he wished that I had. Instead, thinking he needed downtime and that I'd be bugging him, I put up a huge wall between us by drinking and watching Netflix.

Drinking puts a barrier between us and our loved ones—family, friends, and God (both the spiritual one and <u>G</u>ood <u>O</u>rderly <u>D</u>irection). We no longer want to engage in the world. We just want to hide. My son later told me that he couldn't talk to me because he felt like I was completely checked out. I have to agree with him. I was.

After living in Hilton Head for a while, I became very resentful. I was lonely there without my husband and daughter and started blaming my situation on others. I was miserable so I felt I *deserved* to numb my misery with wine! I missed home and the Northeast way of life that I was used to. The people in the South were very different and I had a hard time adjusting. I think my son did too, but I was so self-involved that he became secondary to my issue of wishing I could be home with both my children and my husband, a family like we used to be. Because my son was so busy all the time and had made so many good friends, I wasn't worried about him when I should have been. He also must have missed home, his room, and the life he was used to.

Later, I realized the toll that the pressure of performing at golf was putting on him. He couldn't be a regular kid. Maybe I'm wrong, but looking back, it reminds me of the stories child actors tell of not really having a childhood, the constant pressure to perform can't be easy for a ninth-grade boy. Looking back, I have so many regrets, but my biggest is that I didn't force him to talk to me, tell me how he was feeling. In addition, I was rarely able to spend time with my daughter and missed her terribly. These mistakes haunt me today. Even though I know that hindsight is 20/20, they still haunt me.

When I wasn't busy with yoga or his golf program, and it was after 5 pm, I was drinking. Unbeknownst to me I was spiraling into a vicious cycle of addiction. Alcoholism or Alcohol Use Disorder is insidious—you don't know it's happening until it's got you in a choke hold and you can't get out. It had become a bad habit to open a bottle of wine while cooking dinner and by bedtime, it would be gone. How I got up early, showered, drove my son to school, then took an hour and a half power yoga class every morning, I have no idea.

What Happened

Some people believe they are born alcoholics, whether that is due to genetic disposition or based upon their reaction to liquor the first time they drink. For others there are stages of drinking that lead up to full-blown alcoholism—social drinker, heavy drinker, drinking-is-causing-problems-in-my-life-type drinker, and why-do-I-keep-ending-up-in-rehab-institutions-or-jail-type drinkers. I fall in the second category. I drank normally for years before I started hiding a vodka bottle in my closet.

Like many others, I will probably never know why I have the disease of alcoholism. It doesn't even really matter why. Doctors will point to habitual use as a possible culprit since it doesn't run in my family. The critical point is that today I accept it so that I can do the work to recover from it. Acceptance of the problem (I can't drink safely) and surrender to the answer (stop drinking one day at a time with help from others like me) is crucial to success.

I thought I was really fun when I drank because I became more outgoing. Family told me I was argumentative and belligerent. When it seemed like a great idea to dance on the bar, my friends told me otherwise the next day. The truth was that when drunk I basically turned into my evil twin. She was my complete opposite and I began to really hate her.

I remember one night going to a concert with one of my yoga friends and getting separated from her towards the end of the night. I was so drunk. I was staggering around alone, didn't know where my car was, finally found it, and drove myself home. I was lucky to be alive the next day. That night made me think about how much I had been drinking and how reckless I was becoming. It was after one too many such situations, especially the one where I was too drunk to attend my own birthday party, that as a family we decided I should go to rehab. My friend knew of a good one, so off I went for twenty-eight days.

What I'm Like Now

Five years, a multitude of relapses, and two more rehabs later, I am finally sober. It took a lot of work and even more soul-searching to get there. I have learned that vigilance is key in order for me to stay sober. If I, for one day, forget that I wake up an alcoholic I could relapse. So I work the program, pray, go to meetings, call my sponsor and read literature every day. I am of service to others in some way every day, always telling myself to do the next right thing and that everything else in life will be ok.

I love my life as a sober human being with a fully-functioning mind, body and spirit. I no longer feel depressed and never spend a whole day on the couch watching Netflix. Slowly the little spark inside of me is becoming brighter and stronger. Life isn't perfect—I'm still mending relationships and trying to correct wrongs that I did during my drinking days. Some days it feels like too much, overwhelming. But it also feels like freedom to me—freedom from lies and secrets and hiding. Luckily, I have a very loving family who has stuck by me through thick and thin. I am open and honest with them about my feelings because I have to be. All those years of holding back emotions and stuffing down feelings made me sick. *You can't go around it, you can't go over it, you have to go through it.*

"Since I was a perfectionist, I couldn't even acknowledge my natural gifts. Today, the sober me makes lists of my talents so I can remind myself that if I'm sober, I'm enough."

Lowri Foyle

About Lowri Foyle

Lowri Foyle is a thankful, recovering alcoholic who lives on Fishers Island, New York and Singer Island, Florida with her husband and dog. Her two children are frequent visitors. Lowri is also an accomplished yoga instructor and cake decorator.

Contact Info:
lowrtifoyleyoga.com
lowrifoyle1@gmail.com

Chapter 8

InterFEARence Override

Charmaine Harkins

An Unwelcome Immersion

An immersion into the meaning of life and death started early in my life. At the age of four, my father passed away. His death began the journey of questioning and confusion about the world. Then, at the age of seven, my mother died. I embraced at the time what I now know to be the orphan archetype. The concept of archetypes originated from mythology and developed within the work of Carl Jung and Joseph Campbell as the hero/warrior journey. The orphan archetype is often associated with abandonment and safety.

Although I have loving siblings within an extended family, the bite of those early losses permeated and structured my eventual outlook and formed perspectives that have lasted a lifetime. Despite the context in which death and dying find themselves in our western culture today, I think these early life experiences helped prepare me well and helped highlight and describe the title of this chapter: InterFEARence Override.

Learning to Pivot

Back in the day, I was fortunate enough to participate in several basketball leagues, and during that time, I practiced as though the sport was going out of style. Basketball was a Godsend that helped to process some of the complicated grief I had been experiencing. I discovered this instrumental team sport in the fifth grade and played throughout my childhood, officially withdrawing from the game while in college.

One of the principle rules of basketball involves a term that has recently gained popularity: pivoting. Associated with this word is a standard penalty known as "traveling." When a player does not pivot and moves both feet while handling the ball, an official will blow their whistle and turn the ball over to the opposing side. I am introducing these two basketball terms because they represent how trauma and healing work in my life.

For starters, pivot and travel have different connotations for me now. Little did I know that when I was age four, seven, seventeen, and now sixty-one, pivoting would become a necessary skill to navigate the world. But, of course, I've been doing it all along unconsciously, that is, until the COVID era. So I invite you to notice in your life where you have had to pivot or else receive a traveling penalty. What shifts were necessary to navigate the changing demands, policies, and social mores taking shape?

One of my favorite positive psychology theories these days is "post-traumatic growth." In 2019, my first book, *One Thing At A Time*, was published. One of the chapters is entitled "Redefining Trauma." This concept is expanded upon in more detail in my book. For this contributing chapter, however, I want to highlight specific situations since late 2019. In this chapter, I will describe how the hurdles and ordeals of the last few years, coupled with the most recent revelations from my San Diego trip, make for an interesting example of how pivoting and traveling apply to trauma and healing.

The COVID Years

The COVID years necessitated the need and manifestation for a new lens in my life. The disappearance (deaths) of volunteer activities, organizations, restaurants, friends, travel opportunities, and socializing rattled how I previously came to know my world and my very existence. Like many of us, I was not exempt from deep, dark, and penetrating emotions accompanying a journey into the unknown.

Perhaps some previous experiences here and there during a profound retreat, break-up, illness, or setback all may have helped quell and prepare me for the gravity of month-long quarantines and isolation, including restrictions about bodily decisions. In reality, however, these prior life experiences only scraped the surface of what the COVID phenomenon introduced.

Specifically, what the COVID years provided was an open door into not only my heart and mind but the humanity of others. Also included are the births and deaths occurring in the natural world. There was indeed a mirror of death doulas and portals all around me/us, waiting to be rediscovered during this precious time.

Further, inclusions and exclusions were happening worldwide in my town and life. I was trying to make sense of the adage "truth is stranger than fiction," but it wasn't working. You see, it took a pandemic for me to wake up, take notice and make (self) care more intentional. There was no time, per se. The present became THE time, which in turn permitted the eventual surrendering to the point where I was no longer IN fear. I was doing my best by humbling-up and embracing and facing that fear.

Re-Entry into the World

Sometimes the dark and dreary moments allow us to reach inside and transform our situation(s). Those instances of "inner-safari" work are where the magic and grace happen. You see, I was seriously afraid to fly again. Even when the airline restrictions were lifted, I hesitated. I thought of all that could go wrong and proceeded to convince myself that booking that flight was an unwise idea. Finally, however, I moved through that fear and hesitation just like I have moved through the stages of grief in my past: different emotions, same process.

I recently had the opportunity to venture to San Diego, California (a serious destination bucket-list item since the mid-80s). While there, I learned quite a bit within a short time. Among other things, I discovered the quality of zoo management, the innocence of frolicking sea lions in their natural habitat, the U.S. Navy being alive and well represented in this port city, and the many lessons to be learned about how fear can make or break one's life plans.

I traveled to San Diego because I was invited to attend a conference session when one of the speakers mentioned a long list of virtues and character traits worth considering. Two phrases, in particular, caught my attention, and the proverbial lightbulb was illuminated once again. When lightbulbs appear, I do my best to pay attention. The revelations of "be okay with playing second-fiddle" (pivot) and "have itchy feet" (traveling) were now clear.

I understood that during the pandemic, I was struggling to pivot because I was engrossed with the requirements and regulations of the airlines. My inner traveler, therefore, needed to kick in via a major inward pivot. This bypass was the difference between being unable to physically travel to other countries and instead welcoming introspection once again by rolling with the punches, just as so many others have done during this tumultuous time.

Being in the Moment

Excited from what I had learned at the conference, I embarked on a day of sightseeing. I encountered a poet at a farmer's market named the "Typewriter Troubadour." Each week, his task was to set up his little desk and typewriter and write a poem for a passerby based on what they told him was on their hearts and minds.

After a brief banter about my morning revelations at the conference, he started typing, and voila, I now have a poem that I treasure. For me, this encounter signifies spirit in action. These events unfolded within hours of each other, and my making a connection in the process allowed a healing opportunity to manifest. Where have you let your life experiences unfold, observed what transpires, and recognized that the set of experiences would bring about the most significant healing in your life?

Redefining Trauma, Healing, and Surrender

Today, I am welcoming and embracing the topics of death and dying in a way that brings more joy. Moving from morbidity and melancholy to healing and health is a choice. It also helps to define my spirit more fully, more completely. It's who I am, and assuredly, it is my melody. After all, it is not death I fear; it's all the rules, regulations, and systems surrounding it.

When I hear myself moving toward a pattern that I see as an old narrative, I quickly tell myself, then remind myself repeatedly, that this is only one way of operating, feeling, and thinking. Flipping my own script has assisted with this process and correlates to the information shared earlier concerning positive psychology. Specifically, the movement from a "fixed mindset" to a "growth mindset" sets the tone. Rather than settling on the genetics, predispositions, and heredity story, my resilience is centered upon learning and a term I've recently discovered: pronoia, i.e., the belief that the universe is conspiring in your favor.

I like to question things and practice critical thinking skills.

As a result of my ongoing curiosity, I have been led down rabbit holes that have significantly impacted that newfound lens. It's soul work that asks the questions now, and just like a good wine, the planting, soil quality, elevation, and location are all essential to creating a palatable blend. Yes, I ask a lot of questions. I research. I pray. I like podcasts with diverse topics, hosts, guests, and perspectives; I enroll in courses, classes, workshops, and activities that tap into the power and intelligence of my heart.

I participate in these activities because I feel that when I refrain, I am reacting to life as it is presented to me instead of responding to life as I desire it. I hope this all makes sense, because we are all different on many levels yet very much the same when discussing the soul. After all, we live in the Information Age, where there is so much at our fingertips. Any subject, at any time or anywhere, is available to us.

Community is Key

In addition to surrendering the death and dying story, a near-miss nemesis maneuver that has gained traction in my life during the last two years is the inclusion/exclusion phenomenon. Again, I ask: *Where do I belong now?* Unfortunately, it seems to have intensified and has spilled over into many segments of society.

Yet, there is comfort in working with such an intense feeling and knowing that the only way out is through. Community has also been instrumental during these times. I find ways to evolve in the ever-changing world through my spiritual practices/communities, hobbies, volunteerism, skill development, and other creative expressions.

I look at the world I/we live in and admire the words of a reverend who stood up to his congregation one day a few years ago and spoke out by stating: "At the end of the day, I'd rather be excluded for who I include than included for who I exclude."

What I learned from this and now know is that sometimes keeping ourselves emotionally and physically safe requires some distance, which requires boundaries and discernment. However, when there is no basis or rationale for excluding a person or group, fear rears its head again.

I have found that without a sense of community to provide guidance and direction in my life, there is a void that manages to take hold when I am most vulnerable. When I confront and am conscious of how I shift away from a zone of peacefulness, my energy shifts, and I can auto-correct that vibration.

The adage of "sharing is caring" works well here because when I am able, more often than not, growth is more easily integrated into my life when I have been able to connect the experience with a group or a few individuals. These experiences have been so profound and validating in that they enhance and are very much connected to the compassionate whole of being.

Another aspect of this sacred geometry and quest for meaning is the certainty that nature and wildlife are not exempt from my definition of community. I learn just as much from a rabbit grooming herself in my yard after robbing some lettuce from my garden than I could from a scholar's lecture.

Moving Forward in Life

Distraction has derailed me in the past. However, because I know how these energetic forces influence my necessity for change, I'm more apt to sit with these experiences rather than cast them off or sweep them under the rug. Why? Because these challenges become true opportunities and portals for resisting the resistance. They become a gateway for clearing my lens once again, and new growth spurts are apt to emerge.

For example, I have a daily gratitude practice. My revolution around the sun this year equates to 61. I rhyme my age with a phrase every birthday and embody that throughout the seasons of the year. These are some ways I incorporate some sense of structure (and sense) within the vast multiverse of the 21st century.

All who come into my path are gifts. The discernment arises when we ascertain whether or not that energy is here for our greater good, is meaningful, and will help generate the possibilities of finding our life's purpose. We are all born free by human design to harness our potential. It's about time we started practicing the freedom we were given. It's not a life hack. It's a birthright.

"Sometimes the dark and dreary moments allow us to reach inside and transform our situation(s). Those instances of "inner-safari" work is where the magic and grace happen."

Charmaine Harkins

About Charmaine Harkins

Charmaine Harkins was born in Lawrence, Massachusetts. She obtained her BA in Sociology from Emmanuel College, Boston, and her MA in Community Social Psychology from the University of Lowell. From 1991-1993, she served in the U.S. Peace Corps in the Federated States of Micronesia. Following her tour of duty, Charmaine embarked on a career with the Federal Bureau of Prisons and U.S. District Court. In 2006, she graduated from the Women's Leadership Institute at the Hartford Seminary, and in 2014, she received a certificate of completion in Positive Psychology from the Kripalu Center for Yoga and Health. Her interests are too numerous to list here (yay!). Charmaine currently resides in Connecticut with her cat, Felix. She will forever love her cat, Dusty, who transitioned during the publishing of this book.

Chapter 9

Stages & Stories

Elizabeth B. Hill

For a human with terrible stage-fright, I've spent a lot of time on stages.

Around second grade, we started attending the Kingdom Hall of Jehovah's Witnesses. From the time I was in fourth grade until I was 20 years old, I called myself one of Jehovah's Witnesses. Part of being a Witness is getting up on stage and being part of the Theocratic Ministry School, where girls and women practice for the door-to-door ministry and boys and men read from the bible. I started getting up on the stage to be part of these "talks" when I was a teenager, sometimes playing the Witness, sometimes acting as the "householder" at the door. There were also times when I was part of the program during meetings, sharing my personal stories of living as a witness. There were a few times that I was called on stage with my mom and brother to talk about our lives. My father was, and is, not a Witness, so sometimes we would be asked to serve as an example and share what it was like to be in a household with a father who was "in the world."

Almost every Saturday morning, we would get on the stage of someone's doorstep. Walking down streets, knocking on doors, hoping people would be charmed by our big smiles, rather than slamming doors, screaming at us, or calling the police.

In neither of these settings could I be myself. I always had to wear a dress because that was what was required, and they rarely felt comfortable. I always had to be "on" and make sure my language and words were in line with someone who was "in the truth." Witnesses were "in the truth," while anyone who wasn't was "in the world." As all groups have, there's a certain lingo or language, different words used that are common in that framework, but mean different things, so I needed to use their language and say what was acceptable in that setting.

When I was 20, a series of events made it clear to me that I had to leave the religion. I chose to "leave the truth" in order to save myself. I left many stories and belief systems behind, and began to rebuild my belief systems and fill my mind with new stories and truths.

I stepped off Witness stages and stepped onto the stage at Central Connecticut State University, where I was welcomed into the dramatic arts. And, oh my, did I excel at *drama* there. And not just on stage.

After much confusion, I eventually decided to major in drama and psychology, since I spent most of my time either in the theatre building or having epic mental breakdowns. Having just lost my entire sense of self when I left the religion, I delighted in losing myself even more and becoming other people: Elizabeth Proctor in *The Crucible*, a crazed therapist named Charlotte in *Beyond Therapy*, a pregnant gynecologist in *The Mound Builders*, a lady who thought she was Queen Isabella of Spain but was really locked up in a psych ward, etc...

In my ongoing pursuit to save the world, I decided to get my master's degree in social work, with a focus in community organizing. I began working in the nonprofit field. When I got on stage in my nonprofit work, even though I introduced myself with my own name, I was definitely not myself there either. I was trying to be good, fit in, play a role. I was the virtuous, well-behaved, student who would do what no one else wanted or could figure out how to do. I felt I had to compartmentalize who I was, keep my artistic, passionate side on the downlow in order to be respected and make a difference.

Nonprofits are extremely stressful. Many clients are experiencing trauma and many of the workers are experiencing this trauma with them. The workers often may have traumatic home lives and pasts. Often this is why they desire to get into this field: to be the people that they wished they could find when they were younger. The need never ends. There are always more hoops to jump through, more grant funds to get, grant funds to figure out how to spend, the need to solve immediate needs on the personal and community level, and a need to document it all, to demonstrate need, so you will have resources to solve the need in the future. You have to be able to tell stories about how awful things are, so that you can get more money, while also telling stories about how wonderful things can be, sometimes, to get more money, also. It's like a 7-layer dip of trauma. A tiramisu of trauma, if that's more appealing.

It was very good that I was also teaching yoga at the time. When I taught my yoga classes, I got to step into the role of what I *hoped* I could be. This Zen-like, chill lady, who was bothered by nothing. Inside I felt like a train wreck of anxiety, but outside I was a calm, still, refreshing lake. On the way to teach my yoga classes, I often had to chant mantras in the car to fend off panic attacks. This helped me. I employed the "faking it til you make it" strategy, and it did, in fact, work. Somehow, showing up to embody a calm yogi several nights a week helped me live this throughout the rest of my life, and people began to view me as one of the calmest people they knew.

All of this was good. I am proud of myself for all of these times I stood up on these stages, no matter how scary it felt to do so at the time. I'm also grateful that I got to release some of the stories that forced me to these stages.

A New Stage

I didn't discover that I had a story to surrender around this until I stood up on a stage recently, looked around, and got to experience myself on stage in an entirely different way.

Who was I on that stage?

A Zen, fun, bookish, lovey-dovey dreamer.

I realized on that stage, mic in hand, that for the first time the person I was being on stage, was completely the same on the outside AND the inside.

I was a Zen, fun, bookish, lovey-dovey dreamer on the outside, AND the inside.

I could relax my body.

I could laugh.

I could pause.

I could cry.

I could look over and deeply know the people on the stage with me.

I could look out, catch someone's smiling eyes and smile back.

I could be seen as myself and loved for who I really was.

And it felt really freaking good.

I was completely comfortable in my own skin. And this was not just in the comfort of my home, with my kitty cat, under a cozy blanket. This was out, visible to a room full of people, and a virtual audience online as well.

The Story I Had to Unlearn

The story I had to unlearn was that if I wanted to be successful, liked, and make a difference, I had to be someone else. And I had to put myself in places that felt hard, scary, and dangerous.

I realized in that moment, on that stage, that the way I could make the most difference and help the most people, was to be entirely myself and to show up in places where I felt like it was safe to be entirely myself. I realized I had constructed this whole belief system to keep myself safe.

In order to be loved by God, I thought I had to put on a dress, knock on doors, warn people about Armageddon and be virginal until marriage.

In order to not be shot or have the police called when I walked down streets, I needed to be fun, charming and get the people at the doors to like me.

In order to receive applause, I had to learn a lot of lines, step into fancy costumes, and become someone else.

In order to save the entire world I had to work in the nonprofit system, be smart, do spreadsheets, take on jobs I did not enjoy, or feel comfortable doing.

In order to bring peace to the world, I had to be calm like water, face panic attacks, and have no reaction to anything life threw at me.

But this time, I didn't.

I realized I could walk into this room where I knew almost everyone, where I felt safe, where I knew I was appreciated for who I was, doing work I adore.

I realized I don't have to charm someone with compliments and a smiley face so someone at a door won't go to get their gun or call the police.

I realized I don't have to learn lines that someone else has scripted and someone else has directed, while wearing a fancy costume.

I realized I don't have to show up like cool, tranquil water with no reaction to anything.

I realized I can wear my red dress with a swirly skirt (and pockets!) because today I *want* to wear a dress with a swirly skirt, not because I'm not allowed to wear pants because I'm a girl. I don't have to follow someone else's script or even have a script at all. I can ask these authors anything that feels awesome to ask them because we're cool like that. I can smile out at the crowd and have them smile back. I can cry with them and guess what, they'll probably cry too, cause there's a lot to cry about, both the sad parts of life, and the miraculously joyful.

Through the dream job of sharing my stories, and helping others share theirs, I've gotten to honor and release one story after another. As I often say in my work, when we share our stories, we no longer carry them ourselves, the world carries them with us. These stories lose their power *over* us and can instead be the fuel that *powers* us.

Thanks to all the authors that I've gotten to grow with and learn from, I've gotten to heal through many of my stories. I'm so grateful for all of those writers and readers that have taken a chance on me and our big collaborative dream of a world filled with peace, love, and full expression. I get to make the world a better place right now, as me, in my favorite clothes, and with my favorite people. Unscripted. I finally feel like I can be comfortable in my own skin.

"When we share our stories, we no longer carry them ourselves, the world carries them with us. These stories lose their power over us and can instead be the fuel that powers us."

Elizabeth B. Hill

About Elizabeth B. Hill

Elizabeth B. Hill, MSW, is the CEO and founder of Green Heart Living and Green Heart Living Press. She is the author of *Ignite Your Leadership, Be the Beacon, Embrace Your Space, Success in Any Season, The Great Pause: Blessings and Wisdom from COVID-19, Love Notes: Daily Wisdom for the Soul,* and *Green Your Heart, Green Your World: Avoid Burnout, Save the World and Love Your Life.*

Elizabeth coaches clients on mindful leadership and writing to heal, inspire, and grow their impact in the world. Trained as a social worker, yoga teacher, and ontological coach, she weaves creativity, spirituality, and mindfulness into her work with clients. With over 15 years of experience writing and leading collaborations in the nonprofit sphere, Elizabeth brings a uniquely engaging approach to collaborative book projects. Elizabeth lives in a historic (and hysterical) home in Connecticut with her children, Raven and James.

Author contact information:

www.greenheartliving.com
FB @greenheartliving
IG @greenheartlivingpress
YouTube @greenheartliving

Chapter 10

From Powerless to Powerful

Angelika Kilian

The Powerless Years

I was not always where I am today. Thank God for my journey here. It was tough, from an abusive relationship to not knowing my worth. I struggled with my identity and with pleasing and putting others' needs before me. I was a people pleaser, and that was where I allowed myself to be hurt the most. I always got hurt because I did not stick up for myself. I did not have boundaries, I did not have self-esteem, and I always settled for less.

Growing up without much guidance, I had to learn many things independently. Trust me; they were not the right choices. I did not have a strong relationship with my mom or my dad. My siblings were older than me, and they moved on with their lives with their significant others. I did not have many people to turn to, so I confided in my friends. I would say they were there for me, but not really. Their opinions influenced me, which is one reason I felt triggered about my self-esteem.

Growing up, boys always chose my friends to date instead of me. Every time I liked a boy, he did not like me back. I felt frustrated, ugly, unwanted, and not good enough. Although I was giving them attention and doing things for them to like me, I was degrading myself for their attention. Things went down from there. I started to settle.

I started to settle with every boy that liked me. This was

wrong and unacceptable on my part. I allowed abusive relationships into my life. Verbal, physical, mental abuse, any abuse because I wanted to be with a guy. I wanted to have a relationship. I never thought I deserved better. I cried at night because I needed the attention he was not giving me. Then at 21, I got married. I thought I married a wonderful man that did not play stupid games with my head and emotions. But you know how it is; the beginning is always beautiful.

As life went on, our relationship became a toxic cycle. I could handle it because I was used to being mistreated and thought this was normal. I was repeating the same mistakes with my past relationships, reliving the same treatment, and feeling horrible about myself. I was still a little girl, lost in the trauma of my upbringing. I was a little girl that did not know her worth. A little girl that screamed for attention and was looking to be heard. I did not know healthy boundaries, nor did I have any. I did not know how to say no. This relationship was toxic, unhealthy, and abusive. I also take responsibility and resent my harmful and abusive actions. I didn't know better, nor was I taught better. I just wanted to be with one man for the rest of my life.

My friends influenced me. They were always telling me what to wear or not to wear. They never supported me in things that I wanted to do. I constantly changed for the circle. I hung out to please them and have them accept me. I never belonged to these cliques/groups. I always felt judged and talked about. I was wronged for doing what I wanted. I wanted to do yoga; it was against God. Meditate; it was against God. Write a book about my awakening with Jesus...don't do that; everyone has already done that. I had to second-guess everything I wanted to do. Were they narcissistic? Did I feel put down by other women? What type of shit was that? I always felt like I wanted to impress everyone but myself.

Awakening to Healing

My healing process started when I was involved in a three-car accident on Feb 10, 2021. From this moment on, my life was never the same. When they say things happen for a reason, trust me, they do. During this time of recovery, I slept at my brother's house. I was alone, and I kept many things to myself. It was hard holding it in, so I started to journal. I wrote what I was feeling, what I was thinking, what I was learning, and what I was going through internally and externally. Just wrote. Wrote about my day, about the things that happened to me. I wrote when I was happy; I wrote when I was sad. This felt so good and releasing. I also prayed. I prayed every day and every night. I prayed when I needed answers. I prayed for signs, and then I learned about angel numbers.

I used angel numbers as guidance, as a confirmation of the healing and direction I was going. I would see a number, and I would Google it. A thought would come into my head to see what it was trying to tell me when I was thinking it. For example, try googling the number of the place you live in. You will be amazed.

I went to church every Sunday and used the gospel to relate to my life. Since Jesus is my savior, I looked for the Bible to guide, better, teach, and keep me on track. Jesus went through many turbulences and mishaps meant to break him, and he continued to forgive with love and passion. Forgiveness is the way to freedom. Forgiveness allowed me to move forward with my life with the people that tried to take me down and destroy me. I know that I am a child of God, and no weapon formed against me shall prosper.

Then and now, I wake up every morning before six am and meditate before my day. Meditation would set up my day by allowing me to stay positive, think positive, change my old thinking habits, develop a new mindset, change my perspective on things and deal with a lot going on. It was a go-to when trying to cope with my feelings and emotions. I meditate when I feel any doubt or would get in my head about my thoughts or events, even experience anxiety. You would be shocked at how many different meditations they have on things you are dealing with in your life. It has been said by many that the mind is a powerful tool. Your mind is very powerful.

I also got involved in listening to motivational speakers, which I now find so refreshing. Listening to motivational speakers when I drive first thing in the morning gets me amped up for the day. Listening to experts gets me motivated, excited, and thinking, *I am worth my dreams!* Their words give me the confidence that "I will make it happen" and the courage to "make it happen."

True success only comes when you never give up. You might fail, but you never give up because you believe in yourself. You believe in your Dream. You are your Dream, and it's up to you to make things happen!

God Made Me Break!

God broke me mentally, physically, and emotionally! He broke me from my past trauma and healed me into a new version of myself. He broke me so I could put myself together as the person I always dreamed of being. Oh, did it hurt! The emotional pain, the cries at night, the screaming in the shower for some help. I did it all by myself. I became me. As I am writing this, I am crying. Crying because I am so happy I broke free from the prison that once held me back.

I am so grateful. So grateful for all this pain and this journey of healing. After the shit I went through, I am surprised that I am mentally sane. I thank God for another day to live and inspire people with my story. I love to inspire people and help them, and that's ok. As I met people along the way, I understood myself more. I understood what I was doing wrong, and the tests God was giving me. I understood my challenges and strengths, and how important and strong I am. After all, I could survive without any income raising two small boys.

There was also a learning lesson on conquering and relearning new relationship patterns. I released everything that was not meant for me or holding me back from the life I deserve to live. To reach my highest potential and feel confident and secure with the person I truly am. If I did not release it, God did everything in his power to take it away and remove the people, the things, the environment, and the life that was not meant for me. Damn, I feel free! Free from the shackles that were holding me back. Free from the abuse, the hate, and the constant degrading from the people I trusted and loved.

I realized everything would happen for a reason, allowing me to see how everything happened in divine timing. How amazing to say it was my time. My time for becoming my highest version of myself, the Queen I was always destined to be, and the Goddess I was created to be. The mighty woman who has developed high standards and expectations knows how to communicate my needs, the woman who sees the red flags, and the woman who knows how to address problems, the woman of high standards, and the woman who will not settle for less.

I wanted to become the successful woman that made it. Ultimately, I made it this far in living my dream life. This woman is motivated to succeed, knowing she can have an empire and still give herself time. This woman had relearn patience and did not force things to happen. This woman found peace and happiness in her life. This woman is free and able to do anything she puts her mind to. This woman makes everything and anything possible. As the world-renowned motivational speaker Bob Proctor said, "If your dream is not big enough, dream bigger."

Living as a Powerful Being

As a result of following spiritual grace, I discovered my self-worth at age 32. I offer these personalized realizations to you as a teaching tool for your life:

- Learn what you want and what you don't want.

- Create your standards and hold them with integrity.

- Express how you now require to be treated.

- Understand your value.

- Honor your time as a valuable asset.

- Be clear on what you deserve in life.

- Trust and follow your intuition.

- Honor the joy and peace that arrives in your life.

Yes, I sometimes get disappointed in life, especially being single for over a year, but this was my healing stage. I feel like my highest Queen or Priestess. Motivated and determined. On my A game. Unstoppable until I get what I want. You do not have to know how to do it; you must want it badly and take the first step.

I sincerely appreciate my finances, my old and new friends, the lessons I have learned, and how I now require myself and others to be in a relationship with me. Looking back, I appreciate my struggles, the people there for me, and the help and guidance I received. I am still alive. Do you understand how valuable life is? I was grateful for another day to self-improve and make a difference. I am here to serve a purpose.

One evening, I got dressed up for dinner. I wore a short white, tight dress, with ruffles on the top with one shoulder off.

Dangling, diamond earrings, with sparkling diamond open-toe heels, and a diamond clutch carrying a long-stem red rose. I went to the restroom and met an older woman, Margaret. She said, "You are all dressed up."

I said, "Yes, I love dressing up for myself. I used to save all my nice clothes for special occasions, but every day is a special occasion. I am alive. Live every day as if it's your last. God gave you another day for a reason, for a purpose. So live the life you always wanted."

She agreed with me and commented, "Especially after you've been through so much." Yes, I knew she got it. I knew she went through a lot, and I knew I did too. We both shared a mutual agreement with just a few words. So here I am, spreading women's empowerment and showing compassion for Margaret's story.

I love this; I live for this. When you get the courage to share your story with me, I am here for you, sister. In one way or another, I feel you. I feel your pain, but I also feel your success. It is time to rise, stand tall, and be your Queen. It is my purpose to inspire people like you. It will all be ok, I promise.

I have had many encounters with women, men, and strangers where I see their pain. I approach them and hug them. It's the most incredible feeling that I can be there for someone. A shoulder to cry on. A supportive stranger. We all need empathy one way or another. I love that I emulate my Queen as others look at me, drawn by my beauty. I remind them that we all have a story to tell.

To me, nothing is more beautiful than the support for one another's values and success stories. You are alive and powerful with the potential to be a true winner in your life. But, you may ask, how do I do it? I recommend being your authentic and highest self and not allowing others to devalue you and stop you from living your best life and reaching your dreams. Remember, you are worthy, good enough, and deserve everything you desire. But, having it all starts with the healed you. And, remember, God loves you as well as me.

"You can have it all.
You are worth it and deserve it.
Be the Queen you were born to be and dream big."

Angelika Kilian

About Angelika Kilian

Angelika Kilian was born in Poland and moved to America when she was six years old. Staying true to her Polish roots, she is now a dual citizen of the United States and Poland. Standing at 5' 10" with exotic Polish features, she was quickly scouted over a decade ago by Moet & Chandon to be a model in one of their campaigns. Since then, she has modeled for a diverse group of big names in print and runway. Modeling opened doors to being cast in movies and commercials.

Her greatest passion is entirely off camera, where she is devoted to making the world a better place with her inspiring stories and teachings. She does this for those around her and those she has never met. She is devoted to using her platform to help people and give back to society through charitable causes and shedding light on normalizing mental health and abusive struggles. She believes that being exactly who you are is enough, and you can overcome and do anything you put your mind to.

Author Contact Information:
Angelika Kilian INC
www.angelikakilian.com
Email: realangelikakilian@gmail.com
YouTube @realangelikakilian

Chapter 11
Healing through Divorce
Shell Sawyer

From the outside, my childhood home must have looked picture-perfect. We lived in a quintessential quiet town in a suburb of Connecticut. You know, the kind of town where everyone knows each other, you attended Friday night football games under the lights, and you spent the weekend keeping up with the Joneses.

Recently, I was at a family party, and one of my cousins told me how envious she was of my upbringing. I had a lovely, comfortable home, a pool in the backyard, a loving family, and many friends. I know that childhood sounds ideal! But little did she know I kept a secret. A secret I have hidden from the world. It is time to surrender my story.

Childhood Trauma

That story took me a long time to process, let alone even discuss, but here I am, sharing it with the world because I know there are others, just like me, that need me to release the truth. My truth is, as a young child, a close family member sexually abused me. Someone that I trusted.

What impacted me the most, was that when I brought it up to someone I loved, even though I was threatened not to, they brushed it under the rug—telling me not to discuss it further or mention it to anyone else. So, you can imagine how I felt at this time. Asking for help and not receiving any love in return.

Ignored But Not Forgotten

For years, I ignored what had happened. Ignored might not be truly what I did, but instead suppressed it. I did not think about it. That is, until I got older, maybe in my early twenties, and started having more serious relationships with men. That is when I noticed some issues that began to rear their ugly head. Of course, at the time, I didn't know these issues were related to my early childhood trauma, but now, I do.

You may ask, how did I recognize these things, and what did I do? That is a great question, as the first step to helping yourself is acknowledging that you have a problem. They were glaring when I took the time to notice them. I was looking for someone to love me, but I could not deal with disputes or differences when they arose. I mean, looking back, how could I? That young child looked for help so long ago and didn't get the assistance she needed, let alone the love she deserved—her love was abandoned.

Looking for Love

These abandonment issues stem from my feeling alone and that I could not rely on my loved ones to support or take care of me. I looked for love in all the wrong places, with people who clearly could not take care of me. Sometimes, they couldn't even take care of themselves. My first husband left me in so much debt and put me in dire straits. This led to even deeper wounds. Wounds that made me believe I was unlovable and not worthy.

Even with my self-esteem at the lowest of lows, I still had hope. But, of course, I was looking for love instead of figuring out how to love myself. This was not a recipe for success! That's when I met my soon-to-be husband and father of my daughter.

They say people come into your life for a reason, a season, or a lifetime. I believe he came to me for a reason. Not only did he bring people into my life that showed me love, but he built up my self-esteem. He helped me figure out what was happening and encouraged me to start going to therapy. This was the start of my therapy journey.

The Therapy Road

Therapy has been a process for me. I haven't gone consistently throughout my life—only when I felt it was necessary or desired. I did not know what to expect from therapy initially but felt there was only one way to go...and that was UP! I mean, what could I lose?

Did it help? Absolutely! Did it miraculously change things? Of course not. What it did do was allow me to feel my feelings. When I first started therapy, I didn't know what to expect, but boy, was it good to talk and let it all out for once. It was freeing! Like a bird spreading its wings for the first time after being stuck in a cage. I didn't know what to do with this newfound release.

It allowed me to move forward...move forward with life! But, looking back, I realize, yes, I was freed, but I was not healed. Do we ever heal from trauma? Maybe not, but we have to learn to make space for it.

The Impact of Unhealed Trauma

I hadn't accepted it, at least not yet. When my father died and shortly after my husband asked for a divorce, I crumbled. My world fell apart. I had a tough time dealing with life. My dad was my best friend, my hero, the person I called when something was going well or I needed to talk, and he did the same for me.

That is until he started his battle with Alzheimer's. They call it the long goodbye for a reason.

The man I knew was gone way before he passed away. When Alzheimer's patients depart, you mourn the person you once knew, the man he was before the disease took him from us. I remembered him. But my grieving was cut short as I had a divorce that I needed to get through.

A wise friend once told me, "The only way to the other side is through!" This is true in all things, especially grief. For example, during a divorce, you grieve the end of a marriage and the future you expected.

Back to Therapy

During this time, I decided to start back on the therapy path, as I was not dealing well with what was in front of me. As I had mentioned before, I had not gone to therapy consistently in my life, and only when needed or desired; it was definitely required again at this time.

What scared me about starting along the therapy path again was telling my story once more to someone new. And now, there was further information to share. I expected it to be daunting and maybe slightly embarrassing, but that sense of freedom and relief again overcame me.

I know that therapy during this time was needed and warranted, it got me through this challenging time, but I felt like I needed more. The divorce was overwhelming and lonely. Even though I had a great support system, it felt like something was missing. I blamed myself for my marriage failing.

Feeling Unsupported

I wished I had someone that could walk with me on this journey. Someone who could make sure I was making the right decisions. I mean, this was hard, I was devastated, and some days it was hard to get out of bed, let alone make decisions for my future. But, once I was done and the divorce was final, I took some time to think about what I would have needed that would have made my divorce more successful.

I wanted to help other women going through something similar. I wanted to hold their hand and help them overcome what can be a difficult time in their lives. What could I do?

"You can't stop the waves,
but you can learn to surf!"
Jon Kabat-Zinn

A Professional Path

I researched and stumbled upon the Certified Divorce Coaching (CDC) program. This program was me learning how to surf! A divorce coach is a professional that can guide you through the divorce process. They will help you manage your emotions and prepare you for the road ahead. Holding your hand the whole way.

I enjoyed being part of this program. I met some great individuals that wanted to help others through a difficult time, just like I did. It was very liberating! Boy, do I wish I had a divorce coach along my travels.

While engrossed in the Certified Divorce Coaching Program, I learned about the Certified Divorce Financial Analyst® (CDFA®) designation. Naturally, I was elated, as my background is in finance. I have my master's degree in accounting and have worked in the financial services industry for over 20 years.

The coaching in both programs was EXACTLY what I needed during my divorce. Not only someone who could coach me but could also help me make good decisions because they have expertise in the financial aspects of divorce. The combination of both certifications was a win for my future clients and me.

Divorce is never easy, but if you have the right support, it can be manageable.

How I help others manage their divorce:

1. Gather information and documents

2. Organize financials

3. Talk through emotions

4. Ensure they are getting enough self-care

5. Prepare for meetings with attorneys and/or mediators

6. Determine what they owe and own

7. Share the short and long-term effects of their decisions

8. Contemplate affordability

9. Create a budget for their future

10. Analyze the best settlement option

Not all settlements are created equal. On paper, the dollar amounts may look similar, but there are nuances that a client needs to know to set themselves up for success.

My experience has helped me become more compassionate. I understand what my clients are going through. I want them to be in control and make the right decisions for themselves and their family. You don't have to go through your divorce with any regrets. If you are contemplating divorce, please ensure your financials are in order and you are making the right decisions for your future today.

I have discovered that focusing our attention on the highs and the lows of life is easy. Yet, if our life is truly a journey, then every experience is a teaching experience for what we most need to learn and heal from in our life. Furthermore, there is peace in knowing we can find the courage and tenacity to become role models and service providers for others who have walked our path.

"Do we ever heal from trauma?
Maybe not, but we have to learn to make space for it.
Divorce is never easy, but if you have the right support,
it can be manageable."

Shell Sawyer

About Shell Sawyer

As a mediator, Certified Divorce Financial Analyst® and coach, Shell Sawyer provides divorce-specific expertise, mediation, and supportive coaching through the maze of divorce. She utilizes powerful software to help you see precise data and make data-driven decisions. She encourages others to not to leave their future up to chance. She can help people going through a divorce to find their strength and provides them peace of mind so they can move forward without any regrets.

Author Contact Information:
Finding Strength with Shell
www.findingstrengthwithshell.com

Chapter 12
A Whole New World
Karina Viante-Phelan

Finding True Love

Emotionally I was soaring on a magic carpet ride, just like I saw Aladdin and Jasmine sailing above Agrabah. My heart sang and overflowed with gratitude to be alongside my love. Daily life was filled with peace, playfulness, laughter, and promise for several years.

As this young, nineteen through twenty-six-year-old woman, Nick was the only man with whom I felt safe enough to show my vulnerability. I finally found a Love where I felt treasured. For many years, every morning next to him was like a gift to unwrap. It was one more day to laugh, work, play, and make passionate love with my confidant and best friend. Even the unknowns of our future sparkled in my mind's eye with limitlessness and adventure.

After experiencing childhood neglect, abuse and trauma, I was certain this love relationship was a karmic gift from God, a reward for surviving and surmounting my early years, for being a spiritual warrior, and for holding true to my path. I cherished it; knowing I had found something special and believing not everyone is so fortunate to experience a love like this one.

This relationship was my Cave of Wonders, like the hidden cavern outside of Agrabah, filled with vast riches and immeasurable magic, which could only be entered by an individual whose "worth lies far within"—the diamond in the rough. I already believed that I was here for a Divine purpose and had more polishing to endure before I could carry the Light aptly for others. I also distinctly saw Nick's character assets and a future filled with magnificent potential. As young adults, diamonds in the rough we were!

However, that magic carpet quickly spun out of control and completely unraveled. It left me crash-landed in one of the darkest and most barren pits I'd known. My daily life and the Love of my life both suddenly became unrecognizable. Again, as in childhood, I found myself lost and alone, consumed inside an emotional space of empty blackness. How had I landed in such a painful, unpredictable, dark reality?

Nick had unleashed his inner addict. I didn't know this side of the man I married. I had no idea what sexual addiction was, how it worked or how it was tied to his drug addiction.

The Imposter Arrives

My attention had been focused on independently financing and completing my bachelor's degree as a top student at my university. After graduation, we finally had our beautiful May wedding. However, as the distractions dissipated, I noticed Nick had stopped following his personal path of growth and healing, stopped connecting with his friends in recovery and started treating me very differently.

The impostor looked like my Love, but his energy was uncomfortably different, and his behavior baffled me. On our honeymoon, he went into a fit of rage when he lost his wedding ring, became verbally abusive, and grabbed and shook me uncontrollably. I felt devastated. I had just married him. I couldn't just go home and pack my bags. I had just said, "I do, for better or for worse." Was "worse" supposed to start so soon?!

For Better or Worse

His mounting rage wasn't all I saw changing. Although the internet was pretty new, I caught him sexting online many times with multiple strangers. Among other suspicious activities, I discovered he sent flowers to another woman. But it was much worse; Nick suddenly wanted to use and abuse me for his sexual pleasure and entertainment. At this point, it was clear he didn't care about my well-being at all.

As a formerly sexually abused child, I was confused. Even if you're married doesn't "No" still mean "No?," and what's it called when you're husband forces himself on you? It's your husband, so is that still called rape?

With his unquenchable desire driving him, the imposter set up many scenarios with new "friends" of his in hopes he could share me sexually with others. I didn't drink alcohol or use any mind or mood-altering chemicals, which I believe helped his many attempts be unsuccessful. But my heart and soul felt battered and beaten down.

I was heartbroken, hurt to the core of my being, and confused. How could someone who once cherished me treat me so horribly? Who could I possibly tell to find some answers? What was I doing wrong? How was betrayal and such heart wrenching pain being inflicted again? First, my parents and now my husband?

I was ashamed that my husband, who was meant to love and protect me, was suddenly so cold, uncaring, and disconnected. My head was spinning as my life turned into a waking nightmare.

I was only in my twenties, yet I was reliving the recurring nightmare I had as a child, where everyone I loved and trusted turned into a monster one by one. In my dream and in reality I perfected appearing as though nothing was wrong, smiling on the outside, and becoming visible only when necessary. But skillfully I hid my knowledge of their truth and the depth of my soul from them all. I was standing alone in the blackness again, not knowing how to save myself. But I was resolved that this dark nightmare would never be my children's reality.

The Disappearing Act

The week before Christmas, Nick had gone out one night "to play pool with friends." He didn't return and didn't answer his flip phone. My heart dropped. I thought maybe he got into a fight and was somewhere dying in a ditch, in a hospital alone somewhere or worse—dead. My mind was reeling.

He was missing for an entire week. I couldn't work, eat or sleep. So instead, I spent it on my knees, crying, praying, and feeling sick inside with an inarticulable heartache and nausea. My bootstrap moments were spent calling law enforcement, hospitals, and morgues.

Once the money started disappearing from my savings account, earmarked for our first home, I knew he was alive, at least for the moment. But it was clear he was consumed by the active drug addiction I had only heard stories about. He had been eight years clean up to this point.

I was angry at him, but nothing overrode the pure joy and relief I felt to hear and see his Blazer rumbling up the winding driveway after the longest week of my adult life. Ignorantly, I envisioned his bender as a bump along our path that we would both heal from and come out stronger for on the other side.

Little did I know, this was just the beginning of many benders, many strings of days and weeks of him MIA with me hurting, praying, and begging for his safe return. Each time he resurfaced in police custody and always with a new woman involved as part of his crime or company during his bender.

Reaching for Traditional Help

During his remorseful moments, I checked him into treatment centers. Each time my heart carried the hope of his healing and the subsequent restoration of our relationship to follow.

Internally I felt raw. I envisioned an angel approaching me, gently tapping me on the shoulder, apologizing, and whispering, "Come with me Dear One; there's been a mistake. This is not your life." I could not wrap my brain around all this, and I didn't know how to help him find his way back to the clean and sober version of the Nick I knew so well and loved so deeply.

I felt like I had miserably failed him and God. It was like watching the person you love more than anyone in the world dangling over a cliff. As I strained and struggled to hold on so he could get a foothold or a grip, he slipped through my fingers like sand through an hourglass. I even thought I was the wrong person for him because I couldn't save him from himself.

Even with all the experience I had in the Twelve Step program, beginning with Alatot (for children) and Alateen (for teens), I only knew to be supportive while maintaining certain boundaries. My love was steadfast. I was aware the active addict behavior I witnessed was merely the result of his pain and poor choices, rather than the truth of who he was created to be. But I was in over my head between his self-destructive behavior and his new-to-me insatiable desire for sexual power and excitement.

Digging into My Toolbox

Although I felt overwhelmed at times, I still had a large toolbox packed with emotional and spiritual tools, the support of friends and some family, and several moments of clarity that stood out like a beacon along my path.

Life had always been an uphill battle. I had to fight to survive my childhood and fight for everything I dreamed and/or created for myself. These experiences gave me confidence and skills. But to find the strength I needed, I relied most humbly on my connection with God/Source/The Universe. I cherished this lifelong lifeline and intently sought this comforting connection for guidance.

I took a step back from the chaos of it all and intentionally became the observer in my own story. I wanted the truth, so I asked for it, but I needed to see and listen to the answers the Universe provided so I could choose wisely.

I noted the thoughts and feelings that seemed to just pop into my head. The words of wisdom from others, I gathered like a harvest. The observations of what life looked like with an active addict spouse; I filed those to review intently. Nick's ability or inability to be authentic and honest, I objectively watched it as if it were on a movie screen. These were all gifts of guidance, offering uncomfortable and challenging truths.

Saving My Life

In my search for clues to bring him home safely during his early disappearances, I discovered he had a wife in another country. Much to her dismay, he never divorced her here in the States. I followed Divine guidance to obtain all the legal documentation I could.

After confronting him with a letter from his wife, he continued to lie to me about that marriage, not realizing I knew more and had more evidence than I chose to bring up. He was incapable or unwilling, to be honest about his past, his first marriage, the women he cheated with, and most importantly honest with himself.

During the last treatment center attempt, he blatantly lied again while looking me straight in the eyes. This was a practice the addict in him had made a way of life. I unquestionably knew at that moment that there was no hope.

I refused to live with and bring children into the world with a man who ran from his truth and repeatedly abandoned himself. No one can heal if they refuse to first look honestly at themselves.

Although I feared this unpredictable, rageful, active addict during his next relapse, I still packed my things, scooped up my dog, and moved out. I got a PO box, an unlisted number, a secure storage unit, and an apartment in a different county. I found a lawyer I could afford and did much of the work myself. I won my court case, and my first marriage was legally nullified. I began my new life while grieving daily for my lost Love.

Awakening to a Whole New World

All of those non-glamorous actions honored the truth and worth within me. Step by step, moment by moment, my small efforts and choices accumulated into a daily practice of saving myself. I willingly did the work. I chose myself. I chose my children, who were yet to be born. I chose to step out into a world of all unknowns. I chose to step into looking in the mirror, no matter how scary, and see what lessons I'd gained and what work I needed to heal and grow.

We must understand that while we can plant seeds, be a positive influence, or a compassionate reflection for others; we can only guarantee our own healing and growth. No matter how experienced, skillful and talented any healing facilitator might be—we are always our own Healer and we take ourselves as far as we are willing to go. We have the distinct honor of creating from any point and time a new direction, a new reality, a creation of the life we truly want.

Self-inventory proved to be the ladder to my Healing Cave of Wonders. No matter who we are and what stories or traumas we may have been through, I've found personal inventory to be foundational in self-discovery, self-acceptance, self-forgiveness, and ultimately deep self-love. In the Twelve Step programs, Step Four says, "Make a searching and fearless moral inventory of ourselves."

I was so afraid, I assumed I must not be ready for this step because I did not feel fearless. At my first attempt, barely a teenager, anxiety rushed in, "What if I discover a monster lurking inside of me?" All the real monsters I knew in life had awful and wonderful qualities. Why would I be any different?

It takes COURAGE to look directly, honestly, and objectively at our behavior, our mistakes, and how we think we may have hurt or failed others and ourselves. Courage is not a lack of fear; it is being afraid but choosing to take action in spite of it. It takes courage to be a spiritual warrior and choose to heal oneself.

Healing and Transformation

Once an undesirable behavior or situation is identified through self-honesty and self-inventory, the transformational process can begin. Once we identify the issue, we can free ourselves of the burden of pain, anger, guilt, and shame through forgiveness. The space that carried the heavy, dark burden is freed and cleared to accommodate whatever we choose. The cleared space effortlessly and naturally fills and overflows with the bliss we are created to hold, be it gratitude, love, peace, or joy.

When we have compassion and understanding for the darkest parts of ourselves, it naturally flows to everyone else. The more I love me, the greater my capacity of love for you. The more I understand and accept myself, the more I appreciate your humanity and admire your divinity. The more unified I am within myself, the more I know and emulate that we are all unified.

The healing I want to see in those I love, my community, my

country, and this world, all begin within me.

No matter the injustice or trauma, the answer always begins with a question or a series of questions:

- What is my lesson here?

- What does this situation call attention to within me?

- How can I heal?

- How can I grow?

Finding Answers in Life

It's okay not to have the answers and not to understand what we're going through. We don't have to have all the answers to navigate through successfully. Instead, we need to be willing to ask questions and ask for willingness to remain open to see, hear, and gather the wisdom in our path. As Maya Angelou said, "Do the best you can until you know better. Then when you know better, do better."

This chapter of life taught me that childhood abuse is not the worst pain or betrayal any human can feel, and there is no limit on how many times we might experience a familiar betrayal, trauma or pain until we extract the important life lesson(s) from it. I gained more compassion for people of all ages, realizing we don't know what others are powering through at any point in life.

I discovered that love is not enough to sustain a relationship. It needs honesty, devotion, and dedication from both people involved. Although I watched Nick abandon himself on a large scale, I understood later in my life he served as a mirror for my own emotional limitations. I needed to confront and embrace the part of me that abandoned myself in a desire to feel loved. I found that if I don't understand all of my lessons immediately from a situation, it's okay; it will undoubtedly resurface in my life until I can grasp what it's teaching me. The shocks and extremes of this chapter in my life ignited my passion even more; to savor the sweet moments and live with intention: to seek truth and expansion with abandon.

A Path to Healing

1. **ASK** for guidance and ask the hard questions, "What is my lesson here? How is this behavior/situation reflected in me?"

2. **OBSERVE** the guidance that presents itself through your senses, interactions, and experiences.

3. **BE COURAGEOUSLY HONEST** with yourself. You may need the help of a skilled facilitator, time to yourself to write or sit quietly, or time with a trusted confidant to assist you.

4. **RELEASE** the burdens you carry through FORGIVENESS. The most effective way I've accomplished this is through cellular emotional/spiritual clearing work, much like a guided meditation. It has transformed my relationships and life to such a great degree that I became a facilitator of these gentle and effective processes.

5. **WATCH THE TRANSFORMATION.** The acts of release, surrender, and forgiveness create space for more Light in your life. Your pain is replaced with inarticulable, magnificent treasures like wisdom, beauty, freedom, and bliss. I call these Divine gifts of clarity, peace, and joy our Birthright.

We all have a choice. Any day can be pivotal. We can live from our heart center, loving, accepting, continually growing, and expanding. Or we can hide from the monsters around us and within us, not realizing the confrontation of each monster holds magnificent treasures: gifts of lessons, self-discovery, and expansion.

Are you ready to peek inside your own Healing Cave of Wonders and uncover your Divine treasures? Then, it is time to claim your Birthright of clarity, peace, joy, and abundance.

"The healing I want to see in those I love, my community, my country, and this world; all begin within me. No matter the injustice or trauma, the answer always begins with a question or a series of questions."

Karina Viante-Phelan

About Karina Viante-Phelan

Today, Karina Viante-Phelan is a proud and grateful mother of three (one teen, two young adults). She is happily married, 20 plus years (a story for another book). She is the founder/owner of Divine By Design, LLC; certified healing facilitator and instructor in multiple modalities: Quantum Cellular Healing emotional and spiritual clearing processes, Reiki, ARCH (Archangel Reiki Crystal Healing), Magnified Healing, Psych-K Balancing, yoga, meditation and intuitive spiritual guidance.

With her lifelong background of surmounting emotional, physical and spiritual obstacles, Karina has spent several decades studying and practicing various healing modalities. It is her greatest joy to utilize these gentle and effective practices to facilitate clients in their own healing journey, as well as to teach and mentor facilitators as they enhance their personal skill sets in assisting their loved ones or clients. Long distance and in-person sessions with Karina are available.

Author Contact Information:
www.divine-bydesign.com
201-909-8505
DivineByDesignNJ@gmail.com

Chapter 13

Roller Coasters Are Fun, Right?

Kristie K. Warren

Avoidance of Self

I love roller coasters: the anticipation of the start, the drops that take your breath away, the exhilarating twists and turns. I love it all! Sadly, the roller coaster of healing from trauma is not as enjoyable, nor is it fun to do over and over again! I learned early on that the roller coaster of healing would be a very bumpy ride.

At fifteen I was told by my sophomore year religion teacher that I was filled with anger. I was offended and confused, but immediately laughed him off. He continued, saying I could use the anger for good or it would eat me up. Little did I know that 25 years later I would finally understand what he was saying. Little did he know that when he said that to me, I'd already experienced traumas I'd need to heal from. I held on to the anger he could clearly see radiating within me, because I just couldn't address the feelings.

At that young age, I'd already learned that "NO" didn't mean no, even with a trusted date, learned no matter how much I fought, it was not enough, and learned that I had no value other than what someone could use and then throw away. I'd also already dealt with an eating disorder, abuse, and abandonment. I'd already experienced a loss of self, hatred of what self I had, and learned that no matter how much I raised my voice, I wouldn't be heard by those I really wanted to hear me.

It was no wonder he saw the rage inside me, but I was not willing to understand him. Of course, I was angry! Who wouldn't be? When choice was taken and unwanted actions were put upon me? Showers don't wash off the dirtiness, shame, and guilt. Tears don't change what happened. Telling others brought nothing helpful. I was hurting, yet it manifested as an intense rage inside me that I was incapable of handling for decades.

I felt dealing with feelings was not an option. It hurt too much. I was angry and depressed but would never admit it. I was acting out in so many ways, yet acting like everything was fine on the surface.

Coping Badly

I spent the next few years partying, hurting myself, and avoiding reality. I'd do anything not to feel. Who wanted someone around that felt traumatized? Who wanted someone around that complained? No one! I did all I could to be the fun girl. I shouldn't admit it, but those times were just fun. That's the problem with poor coping skills, many are quite fun and a great distraction from reality. I now know even my suffering was a vice I didn't want to let go!

After college and having a family, the improper coping continued. The self-hatred never seemed to go away. The anger with others became a regular occurrence. I shopped, ate, drank, and had no self-awareness that the excess I kept myself in was coming from an intense lacking within. I had no idea who I was. I did know that there was no amount of concerts, parties, or purses that could fix my aching spirit, but I still did it all to fill my void.

I fell into depression again. Carrying the baggage from my past was making my life and my family's life unbearable but when would I put that baggage down? When would I be able to finally heal? Well, a new kind of trauma would finally force me to address my past!

No More Roller Coasters?!

At age 40, I suffered a car accident that caused a traumatic brain injury. I was angry, but this time I didn't need to be told by a former teacher. It was all I thought about. This time, though, I realized that perhaps my teacher was right all those years ago. Maybe I could use it for good and fight to be better instead of just fighting the world. I knew that fighting for myself was the only way through it.

The irony of not feeling heard in my life would play out with this injury. My voice was taken, literally. I had to learn how to speak again, to walk without falling over, and new ways of doing basic tasks I'd always taken for granted. My neurologist told me I'd need to get into many different therapies as a result of my injury. I understood the need for speech and physical therapy, but why psychotherapy? When he said I couldn't ride roller coasters again, I was devastated, but how would psychotherapy change that? Sadness over having to avoid theme parks was such a focus for me, but it wasn't where my focus needed to be. Again, I was avoiding reality once again.

It took so long to find a therapist that could deal with my injury, but I found a great one. She took me and my issues on with so much integrity and empathy. I started telling her about the trauma of the accident and how horrible I felt. Now, as I say I sat there telling her, I really couldn't *say* much. I stuttered and slurred and sat there day after day physically hitting my head trying to get the words out of my brain. I would cry and complain that this was the new me and was the messiest I'd ever been in my life. It was such a dark time in my life. There were so many days I wished for death.

I was so angry with the man who hit me with his car, with God, and with those closest to me that abandoned me. I lost so much. I was angry with anyone that would tell me just how awful I sounded. It was awful. How and why did this happen to me? How would I come through this? I had no idea, but knew I had to just keep going.

Mirror Mirror on the Wall

It was about two years into therapy that I finally understood why my neurologist sent me. I realized that healing my past was the only way to heal my brain. To look back on my life experiences and deal with the feelings was incredibly hard. I didn't like having to dig it all up. Who wants to remember the trauma? I coped improperly to forget those things since I was a teen! I knew I couldn't do any of that to cope this time, though. I had to address all that happened to me, process all my feelings constantly, and hold a mirror up to myself in a way I'd chosen not to do all my life.

Holding onto trauma is suffering in itself and I seemed to find comfort in that suffering. My own suffering was a vice and it seemed I enjoyed it in some sick way. Realizing that was a sad epiphany and I knew I needed to change. I wanted that suffering to end and was willing to do the work. I just had no idea how much work it would take. Holding a mirror up to yourself is humbling and scary. Seeing what was inside triggered all the insecurities and unhealthy coping skills that I'd mastered in life. If hating myself was an Olympic sport, I'd win gold. I knew I didn't want to live like that anymore. I could turn my gold medal in!

I decided to dive in and dedicate myself to healing. I decided that no matter how my life played out I would need to change my entire being. I realized that my old life before my accident wasn't something I wanted back. I didn't want to carry the hurt and trauma with me as I healed my brain. I didn't want to cope improperly. I knew going forward with a new world view was the only way to get change and only I could control that view.

I learned I didn't have to have the last word, didn't have to fight those I felt wronged me, and didn't have to let anyone else understand me. If someone doesn't understand me, that's on them. That didn't mean I didn't have challenges with others, it just meant I finally understood that I needed to be ok with me and me alone. I wasn't responsible for others' actions and I didn't have to depend on their acceptance to feel okay.

I also committed to trying things that I heard healed others. Therapy made me confront feelings I didn't know I had. Meditation made me confront the peace I'd always yearned for but never had. Prayer made me confront feelings of inadequacy and a lack of acceptance that only God could give me.

One Minute at a Time

I realized the work I was doing was making a difference. I realized that new traumas I'd experience could be met differently. It was then that the roller coaster of life would take a new turn. I was told my marriage of almost 25 years would be ending. I was a mess, but knew I had to deal with it head on. The feelings about the divorce wouldn't be realized until about a year later. I'd been so good about avoiding feelings my whole life that it was a habit. I'd finally moved towards healing and now old habits were showing up again? Yes. Yes, they were. This was a topper! How could I get through this? How would healing come from this trauma? Well, good readers, it is only through hell that you can come out the other side. So, I did the work again.

I'd spent so long hating myself for what others did to me, for not feeling heard, for not being able to cope properly. I know how many mistakes I made. The guilt of that turned into anger and improper reactions. I knew that this divorce would force me to look at all of that and even deeper into myself. Even though it was scary, I knew I could do it. And I also knew I needed to forgive myself to move forward. For you see, I was holding on to the hurt and not coping, which affected others and for that, I had to forgive myself for not doing better.

I knew that I had to take healing one day at a time, or really, for me, it was one minute at a time. I knew giving my hurts, habits, and hang ups over to God was the way forward. I knew that I needed to accept the things I couldn't change, courage to change things I could, and knowledge to know the difference. Releasing the baggage would lead to even more resilience and a peace I craved.

Trying to live one minute at a time has been the key to moving forward. The saying, "The rearview mirror is small for a reason," has always resonated with me. As much as I had to look back in therapy to heal, I also started realizing that the front window is much larger. I could look forward and build the life ahead of me that I wanted! I began to understand that the struggles of the past were there to remind me of how far I've come, not how stuck I had been.

You Are Worthy

In trying to heal my various traumas, I have learned that feeling worthy is a major issue. I work with others who have suffered traumas and love giving them encouragement to be courageous in their fight. I would be the first person to tell them they are worthy, but couldn't feel it myself. I've spent a lifetime being hard on myself and changing that has been terribly difficult. To be honest, I still work on it every day.

Healing from traumas, whether physical or emotional, can be agony. It takes work and dedication. Healing isn't linear. It isn't a constant, upward trajectory. It has more twists and turns than Space Mountain! I want you to know, though, that you, and I, are worthy of that healing roller coaster. You are worthy of goodness in your life. Whether it's abuse, assaults, or any other trauma, know it isn't your fault, and that you are worthy of moving forward without anger, depression, anxiety, self-hate, and coping badly.

Traumas can strip you of your worth. They strip you of trust, comfort, and a sense of self. They can attempt to change your spirit. Yet, healing through those traumas can give you a renewed spirit, a stronger sense of self, or even a new sense of self that you'd never had, like in my case. Healing can glue those pieces back together you may feel were lost. Healing is work but you can do it! No matter what, you can get through it.

Working on yourself through therapies, meditation, or religion are all good options. Try new things to heal. Give yourself permission to feel every feeling you have. Give yourself permission to break down. Don't fight it. You will get up and thrive one day, I promise! Addressing your traumas doesn't give them power over you. It gives you power *over* them. In the end, you can work through all the pain, guilt, shame, and frustration and come out of it a stronger, more authentic you. You are worth it!

Rearview Mirror Lessons

Looking back on my healing journey, I realize just how strong and resilient I am. I realize that it was my resilience and my willingness to release the anger and hurt that would help me move forward in life.

Moving forward, though, doesn't mean I'm completely healed. Healing is a journey and a process that I think won't ever truly be over. We evolve. We change. We experience new hurts. What I can say about the hurts of the past is that I am who I am because of all I've experienced. I like me now. I know I screw up. I know I say the wrong things whether it's my brain injury or not. I know I still have work to do. I do know, though, that I can do the work and it will get better.

As I decided to write of my healing, I asked someone close to me if they thought I was an angry person. They said no. I love that. I worked so hard to remove the chip on my shoulder I'd carried for decades. I worked hard for that release.

It is with that hard work, strength, and passion that I now use my experience to benefit others. I share my story and my experiences internationally, train others that have traumatic brain injuries on coping strategies to improve their lives, and have had my writing published in a best-selling book. I focus on volunteering my time to improve the lives of others and help them work through their struggles. By doing that, I also keep working on mine.

And by working on mine, I find a sense of peace on this roller coaster of life. I know that no matter what you face on your roller coaster, you can find peace too. Just gotta get through those ups, downs, twists, and turns.

"Therapy made me confront feelings I didn't know I had. Meditation made me confront the peace I'd always yearned for but never had. Prayer made me confront feelings of inadequacy and a lack of acceptance that only God could give me."

Kristie K. Warren

About Kristie K. Warren

Kristie K. Warren is a mother of two amazing adult children, has a wonderful son-in-law, and is expecting her first grandchild. She is a passionate traumatic brain injury survivor advocate and speaker, who believes anyone can soar to greater heights than they even thought possible. She is a best-selling co-author of the book *Trauma to Triumph: Stories of TBI Survivors and the Vital Role of Post-Acute Care*, where she wrote of her TBI recovery. She trains and mentors other TBI survivors on strategies to work within their new limitations, volunteering with the non-profit BEST, Brain Education Strategies Technology.

She sits on California's Traumatic Brain Injury Advisory Board, where she advises state leadership on policies, programs, and services impacting people with TBI. She sits on the Public Policy and Funding Committee, which expands systems to support TBI survivors that intersect with homelessness and domestic violence. She co-chairs the Brain Injury Survivors Committee, which is focused on expanding outreach and support for those who have suffered brain injuries. When Kristie is not writing or giving her time to help others, she can be found on the sand at Lifeguard Tower 19 in Newport Beach.

Author Contact Information:
Email: OurProjectSperanza@gmail.com
Instagram @Project.Speranza

Chapter 14

Breaking the Cycle

Bryanne Weightman

I was raised by my father, my beautiful, wise, spiritual, alcoholic mess of a father. To understand how my father's struggles impacted me, I must start at the beginning of my parent's relationship. My mother was 21, and my father was 23 and studying in the seminary to become a protestant clergyman when I was born. Former 70s wild children, my mother recalled that she envisioned a different life with my father, a music man who toured regionally with his band.

Instead, when my father received "the call that he was unable to ignore" from God, he transferred into the seminary to become a reverend and serve as God's messenger, much to my mother's chagrin. When I was three, my father was ordained an elder in the church and assigned his first parishes. We moved to rural Pennsylvania, farm country, and began our new lives. Immediately my mother, Mary, then 24, with two small children (my brother Grant and me), began to rebel against her new wholesome life.

My Mother's Discontent

Mary reconnected with a former high school friend who had served a stint in jail. She began to frequent his family's home, where he lived with his mother and younger siblings. According to my father, she began to "run wild" and then made terrible choices. Mary became pregnant, but not with her convict friend's baby; no, it's much worse. Mary became pregnant with her friend's younger brother Joe's baby. Mary was 24. The boy Joe was 14. Mary had violated our family by cheating. She had stolen the childhood of this boy, Joe. Her legacy of destruction in people's lives had only just begun.

My father decided to be a good Christian man, swallowed hard, and chose not only to forgive Mary, but to raise this innocent child as his own. As his older sister, my brother Eric was a beautiful blond-haired, blue-eyed charmer whom I adored. Our family lasted for four years like this until Mary decided to run away with the boy Joe who got her pregnant. He was now 18, and Mary chose to run away to Virginia Beach with him, and she took my brother Eric with her.

As I got on the bus for second grade that October, my parents met me at the door. "Mommy won't be here when you get home from school. She's no longer going to live with us, and she is taking your brother Eric with her." That was the explanation I got at the time, and then they pushed me out the door to catch my bus to school. I was devastated. My father began to self-medicate with alcohol.

My Mother Returns

I didn't see my mother or brother again until the following Spring when she drove to my grandmother's house to visit for Easter. By then, Mary was pregnant again by my now stepfather, Joe. She looked at me and spoke about me to my grandmother as if I wasn't in the room. "Look what her father's done to her. He cut off all her hair, and she's getting fat." She didn't know that my father had tried unsuccessfully to braid my hair many times. He used to comb it every night, but it was too unruly. Finally, he took me for a haircut, and I begged him not to cut my hair off. They all lied to me and said they would not cut it off. When I left the salon,

I had a pixie cut. I was devastated.

PopPop and Love

My PopPop (paternal grandfather) moved into our home in the winters to help my father care for my brother Grant and me in my mother's absence. He was the voice of calm and stability. He was love and was always cooking some interesting concoction in the kitchen. One particular favorite was his baked beans, hot dogs, mustard, and cheese casserole with a cornflake crust—a favorite for the kids, despised by adults.

Pop saw that we were bathed, clean, fed, and dressed for school each day while my father soldiered on and served his churches selflessly. This household of men tried their best to raise a little girl but ultimately succumbed to what seemed most natural and raised me no differently than my brother. I was told I could be anything. What type of doctor would I be? Where would I attend graduate school? "The sky is the limit."

Becoming a Female

There was no acknowledgment of how to be female until I was about 12 years old. My father collected me one summer from the woods and told me to wash my dirty feet up because we were going to New York City tomorrow. When we arrived in NYC, my father and I sat on a bench, watching people in the new heeled shoes he had just bought me. He was looking at the people passing by, intently studying them. He gave me a lesson on how to "read people" and then darted up and told me to follow him. We were behind a woman walking in an "attractive female way." My father was trying to show me an example of a female gait as he looked for attractive females for me to mimic.

We walked at a distance behind this woman, and he pointed out the mechanical components of her walk. "See how she swings her hips side to side a little when she walks? Try that...Don't swing your legs to the sides as you walk; your legs should go straight in front of you...Watch how she swings her arms." We concluded the day with a stint at the make-up counter of some fancy department store, where they put me in clear mascara, a little pink blush, and some eye shadow. There was always alcohol at lunch and dinner with my father, but this was a day largely unmarred by his drinking.

My Father's Addiction

As I got older, my father's drinking became more of an issue. I remember parishioners coming to the door at night and me praying that they couldn't tell he'd been drinking. He was the only parent in my home, the only breadwinner, and my future directly depended on him keeping that job. People let many things slide out of pity for the single man raising two kids alone. I'd fear him picking me up from sports practices in the evening, knowing he'd be at some stage of intoxicated, and we had a 40-minute drive home from school.

At 15, my PopPop passed away peacefully in our home. With him gone, there were no longer any checks and balances in the house for my father's alcoholism. Although he was a "functional alcoholic," his lack of presence increased as he stole away in the house, likely drinking. Towards the end of high school, I remember him coughing up blood. I now know those were rupturing esophageal blood vessels that went to his liver circuits, put under too much pressure from the damage to his liver.

Life's Ups and Downs

I went to see my mother and her new family two days a month, always with my father encouraging us to take the good from her but leave the bad. Dad was constantly pushing me higher. "Don't be like me, baby, do what I say, not what I do." My father successfully got me through undergraduate and graduate school despite his drinking. Then, as I began my doctoral program, I got a call that he was in the hospital with cirrhosis of the liver and experiencing liver failure. Miraculously, he was one of the rare percentage of people whose liver spontaneously recovered, and he tried his best to be sober and stay away from alcohol.

Unfortunately, he hit a deer on his motorcycle and had some compound bone fractures. This led to doctors prescribing him narcotic pain pills freely. This was when doctors thought prescribing pain pills while you were in pain wouldn't cause addictions. They were wrong, and we know this contributed to the opioid epidemic we currently experience. The opioids spiraled my father into a cycle of addiction. The addiction put his already feeble liver over the edge.

My Father's Final Years

Only a couple of years before he passed away, obviously struggling with the demons of addiction, my father gave a beautiful convocation at my doctoral school graduation. He had completed the "sacred task" of parenthood. He would say it had nearly killed him, but if done well, parenting leaves us with almost nothing left of ourselves because we have given it all to our children.

At age 31, I received a phone call that no one wanted. I was told I needed to come home immediately because my 54-year-old father would not make it. So I drove to the hospital at six am with a police escort at lightning speed. I got to the hospital in time to see my father lying in an ICU bed with blood running out of his nose onto a gauze and his heart being pumped for him on life support. His hepatic liver portal blood supply had ruptured due to liver disease. As a result, he had "bled out internally." I held his hand and prayed with him as the life support went to zero.

My Life of Service

At 31, I was married with three beautiful children. I was a doctor, owned my own home, and led a life of service to others. I worked on medical missions and served our country in the United States Army. I ran a homeless shelter medical mission and was actively advocating for others less fortunate than me. When my father passed, he told me that my faith was the greatest gift he had ever given me. As I began the grieving process that comes with losing the sole person who raised you, I realized that somehow, despite all of the atrocities that had happened in my young life, my soul had made it through unscathed.

Growing up as a pastor's daughter in the church, I was always surrounded by the presence and concepts of God, an omnipotent, omniscient, omnipresent being. Prayer and talking to the spiritual presence of Christ in my life was as natural as eating breakfast. I realized that my inner monologue spoke to God and Christ, instead of just my inner self, all the time. I thought in "we's," for example: *What are we going to do today?* Or *Good Morning, Lord God, please walk closely with me today so we can accomplish all the things you want through me.*

My Spiritual Journey

I began to explore my own spirituality and learn about my goals for spiritual development, such as my life's purposes. I learned about different spiritual modalities. Through a shamanic healing session, I learned about the spiritual protection I received as a child. I learned that children's souls have a keeper or a protector. It was revealed through the shamanic session that my soul had passed from my mother's care to my grandfather's

(PopPop) care when I was seven.

My PopPop was given the sacred soul's task of preserving my soul's innocence so that I could complete my soul's missions as an adult here on the Earth plane. That made perfect sense looking back. PopPop stepped right in where my mother left off and was the embodiment of love in my childhood. Yet, I never knew at the time that he was also protecting my soul from harm. God or the Divine or Spirit had orchestrated every step of my childhood to protect me. I simply had to have faith enough to experience and listen to it.

When my father passed, a colleague of his wrote an email that he had had a dream in which my father relayed to him that he had had a difficult life review, but had made it through successfully. As a result, I became more spiritually aware and began to encounter a spiritual awakening of my own. I met with clergy, spiritual teachers, and people from many different traditions as I understood what was happening to me. I was developing an awareness that the veil between the spiritual and physical worlds is very thin.

My Greatest Knowing

Despite my father's flaws, he walked me towards a life of service and an ability to actualize my soul's purpose. I overcame my father's alcoholism and my mother's abandonment. Throughout all this, my father instilled in me an ability to see the world as communion with Spirit. This spiritual foundation has shepherded my every decision and action. I can't recall a time when Christ's energy was not present for me. For sure, both of my parents had demonstrable flaws, but I have taken the best from their influence on me and forgiven them.

If you are reading this chapter and have struggled with parents with significant flaws, I invite you to see them as teachers for you on your soul's journey in this lifetime. So often, the members of our soul family who love you the most will incarnate into this lifetime to play the most challenging roles in your life. You chose your parents to be the most significant catalyst for your spiritual growth. When you can shift to seeing them as a teacher for you, you can move into unconditional love (acceptance without judgment). By no means do you need to condone their actions, but by forgiving them, you are healing yourself.

"This household of men tried their best to raise a little girl but ultimately succumbed to what seemed most natural and raised me no differently than my brother. I was told I could be anything.
What type of doctor would I be? Where would I attend graduate school?
'The sky is the limit.'"

Bryanne Weightman

About Bryanne Weightman

Bryanne Weightman has lived a life of service and is married with four beautiful children. She is a doctor, has worked on medical missions, and served in the United States Army.

GREEN HEART
LIVING
— PRESS —

Green Heart Living Press publishes inspirational books and stories of transformation, making the world a more loving and peaceful place, one book at a time.

Whether you have an idea for an inspirational book and want support through the writing process—or your book is already written and you are looking for a publishing path—Green Heart Living can help you get your book out into the world.

You can meet Green Heart authors on the Green Heart Living YouTube channel and the Green Heart Living Podcast.

www.greenheartliving.com

Green Heart Living Press Anthologies

Ignite Your Leadership

Answer the Call

Be the Beacon

Trauma to Triumph

Embrace Your Space

Redefining Masculinity

Success in Any Season

Transformation 2020 Companion Journal

Transformation 2020

The Great Pause Journal

The Great Pause: Blessings & Wisdom from COVID-19

Made in United States
Orlando, FL
24 February 2023

30362680R00083